W9-AYF-283

PENGUIN BOOKS

FIRST AID FOR CATS

Bruce Fogle, DVM, runs a veterinary practice in London and is a founding manager of the Emergency Veterinary Clinic, London, the first facility of its kind in Britain. He is the author of more than twenty books on pet care, including *The Cat's Mind* and *Know Your Cat* and is a regular columnist for *The Daily Telegraph*.

First Aid for
CATS

WHAT TO DO WHEN
EMERGENCIES HAPPEN

Bruce Fogle
DVM

Illustrated by Amanda Williams

PENGUIN BOOKS

PENGUIN BOOKS
Published by the Penguin Group
Penguin Books USA Inc., 375 Hudson Street,
New York, New York 10014, U.S.A.
Penguin Books Ltd, 27 Wrights Lane, London W8 5TZ, England
Penguin Books Australia Ltd, Ringwood, Victoria, Australia
Penguin Books Canada Ltd, 10 Alcorn Avenue,
Toronto, Ontario, Canada M4V 3B2
Penguin Books (N.Z.) Ltd, 182–190 Wairau Road,
Auckland 10, New Zealand

Penguin Books Ltd, Registered Offices:
Harmondsworth, Middlesex, England

First published in Penguin Books (U.K.) 1995
Published in Penguin Books (U.S.A.) 1997

1 3 5 7 9 10 8 6 4 2

The Cats Protection League would like to state that although this book is
helpful in the diagnosis and treatment of simple feline ailments, the League
does not accept responsibility for the content. If a cat becomes ill, owners
should *always* seek the advice of a veterinarian.

LIBRARY OF CONGRESS CATALOGING IN PUBLICATION DATA
Fogle, Bruce.
First aid for cats: what to do when emergencies happen/Bruce Fogle;
illustrated by Amanda Williams.
p. cm.
Includes index.
ISBN 0 14 02.5542 7
1. Cats—Wounds and injuries—Treatment.   2. Cats—Diseases—Treatment.
3. Veterinary emergencies.   4. First aid for animals.   I. Title.
SF985.F64   1997
636.8'08960252—dc20   96–34002

Printed in the United States of America
Set in 11 ½ / 12 ½ pt Palatino

Contents

CONTENTS

Introduction

Cats are living longer than ever before, and for logical reasons: routine inoculations have brought many infectious diseases under good control; nutrition has improved; and we cat owners have a better understanding of the risks of the 'urban jungle'. More than ever before many cats lead long and contented indoor lives free from the risks of traffic accidents, fights with other animals and trauma in general. When I was a child a cat's life expectancy was about ten years. Today it ranges from thirteen to twenty years depending, at least in part, on the breed of your feline. That is an amazing success story.

Today, most cat owners do not question whether good veterinary attention is nearby. That fact is taken for granted. What does puzzle or even worry owners is whether their cat's problem justifies the time and expense and often, for the cat, the trauma of a visit to the vet. Cats sometimes have the annoying habit of pretending they are healthier than they really are. This book shows you how to give first aid in emergencies. It also helps you decide when and if your cat needs professional medical attention.

The book is divided into four parts. Part One describes what to do first when an emergency happens; how to restrain a cat, check its vital functions, maintain life, apply bandages and splints and tourniquets and safely carry the cat. Practice the instructions in this section as you read them, while your cat is robust and healthy. Understanding this section will enable you to act efficiently and knowledgeably in an emergency.

Part Two explains, step by step, what to do when the immediate crisis is over. If you are not sure about the seriousness of the situation, this section will help you decide whether veterinary help is needed and, if so, how quickly you should seek it. If you find something that is potentially life threatening or if what you find suggests that the cat is in hidden pain, these facts are highlighted with easily recognizable symbols.

Part Three describes what to do in obvious emergencies. Emergencies are listed in alphabetical order, from **Aggression** through **Choking** and **Drowning** to **Poisoning** and, finally, **Vomiting**. For each emergency there is a description of how to give first aid and a chart to help you make the sometimes difficult decision about whether you should go to the vet as quickly as possible, whether you can wait until later in the day or until the next day, whether you should simply telephone your vet for advice, or can proceed solely with treatment at home.

Part Four describes how you can minimize risks to your cat, how to give medicines and how to prepare a first aid kit.

Acknowledgments

Veterinary medicine is a curious profession. A vet is expected to treat virtually any emergency that arises in any species of animal. This is one of the satisfactions and challenges of the work, and after practicing veterinary medicine for a quarter of a century, I have seen my allotted share of emergencies.

At the same time, veterinary medicine is a highly specialized profession. Some vets concentrate on specific species – cats or horses for example. Others specialize in specific fields such as orthopedics, ophthalmology or dermatology. Emergency medicine and critical care is one of these specific fields.

When reading this book, you will come across some excellent advice and suggestions. When you do, more often than not they have probably come from Dr Suann Hosie of the Vancouver Animal Emergency Clinic in Vancouver, British Columbia, Canada. In both California and British Columbia, Dr Hosie has gained more experience in emergency medicine and critical care than virtually anyone else in Europe or North America. I asked Suann, a schoolmate from the Ontario Veterinary College, to read this book before I sent it to the publishers and she offered constructive advice on just about every single page. My appreciation is enormous.

PART ONE

THE ESSENTIALS OF
FIRST AID

What is First Aid?

The objectives of first aid are to:

- Preserve life
- Prevent further injuries
- Control further potential damage
- Minimize pain and distress
- Promote recovery and repair
- Transport the cat safely to the veterinarian for professional care

Do not waste time trying to make an accurate diagnosis. Assess the situation quickly. Is the cat in further danger? Are you in danger if you try to help? Catch and restrain the cat and remove it from the risk of further harm.

Assess the cat's condition. Look for obvious life threatening signs. When necessary, give emergency first aid on the spot. If someone else is available, they should get help by telephoning a vet and arranging to transport the injured cat.

An emergency is not the best time to ask your vet to make a house call. Whenever possible, it is almost always better to telephone the vet and take the injured cat to the nearest professionally equipped veterinary clinic.

What to Do First: The Basics of First Aid

When emergencies happen, carry out a quick physical examination of your cat. It is important to do so if you are to be accurate in your decision making and treating of emergencies. While your cat is fit and healthy, carry out these procedures:

- Restrain the cat
- Check breathing rate and rhythm
- Check heart rate or pulse
- Look for signs of shock

Do not try to carry out an examination in one session. Remember to reward your cat's obedience with a food snack, touch or praise. Give a reward after each step.

After you have carried out a brief but thorough emergency examination of the cat, you may need to administer first aid. The basics of first aid are:

- Artificial respiration
- Heart massage (cardiopulmonary resuscitation, or CPR)
- Cleaning wounds
- Applying bandages, splints, tourniquets and Elizabethan collars
- Lifting and transporting ill or injured cats

In genuine emergencies, remember that your objectives are to save life, prevent further injury, pain or distress, and to help promote recovery.

HOW TO EXAMINE YOUR CAT

The better you are at understanding how to examine a cat the better you will be at giving first aid and making decisions

4

about the seriousness of a situation. Practice these steps on your own cat but do so for only short periods at a time. Some cats resent being handled. Remember to reward your cat's willingness to be examined with tasty snacks, petting or praise. Give a reward after completing each step.

RESTRAINT

Use as little restraint as necessary to carry out your examination. Too much restraint upsets most cats and makes them uncooperative. An injured cat is likely to lash out with teeth and claws. Protect yourself by wrapping a frightened cat before lifting and examining it. If you are bitten or clawed always seek medical advice.

1. Approach the cat calmly. Talk to it reassuringly. Initially, avoid intimidating and, to the cat, threatening direct eye contact.
2. While still talking, check the cat's expression to determine how frightened it is. Stroke the relaxed cat on the side of its head then slip your hands under its body and pick it up. To examine a calm cat hold it as shown in Figure 1.

Fig. 1: Holding a calm cat

Gently but firmly grip the cat's head from under the chin. Apply light pressure against the cat's body with the elbow of your free hand while you carry out your examination with that hand.

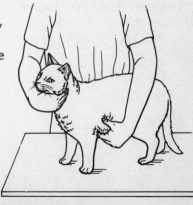

EXAMINE

3. A frightened cat resists handling and tries to escape. Eliminate escape routes. Speak and move calmly. Avoid any sudden gestures. Place a blanket, towel or sheet over the frightened cat.

(If your cat is frightened by your approach do not use it to practice your examination skills on. Use another more amenable cat.)

Fig. 2: Restraining a frightened cat

a. Place a blanket, towel, sheet or article of clothing over the cat's entire body. Wrap the cover under the cat ensuring that it cannot lash out with its claws.

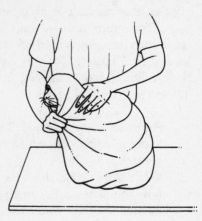

b. Gently unwrap the cat's head. Continue to speak soothingly. Proceed with the examination only when the cat is calm.

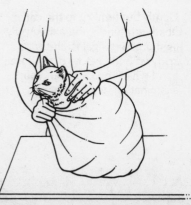

MONITORING BREATHING

Your cat normally breathes between ten and thirty times a minute. Kittens and young cats breathe more quickly than mature ones. Cats normally have very subtle chest movements when they are resting. Purring makes it even more difficult to assess accurately the respiratory rate. Calculate and record your cat's normal rate of breathing.

Cats pant when agitated, to eliminate excess heat, or when they are in pain. Panting is much more rapid than normal breathing. When calculating the normal breathing rate of your cat, monitor only regular breathing through the nose.

1. While your cat is relaxed, watch how many times it breathes in twenty seconds. Only count breaths in or out, not both. Multiply by three to find the rate per minute.
2. If your cat has a fluffy coat or breathes so lightly that you cannot see any chest movement, hold a piece of tissue in front of its nose and count the number of times the tissue moves in twenty seconds. Multiply by three to find the rate per minute.
3. Alternatively, place your hand on your cat's chest and feel for each breath taken in over twenty seconds and multiply by three.

Observe your cat's nostrils. They are motionless during normal breathing but flare slightly with each inhalation when extra effort is needed to breathe. Flaring nostrils are a clue that your cat is not well.

TAKING THE PULSE AND MONITORING THE HEART

A cat's resting heart rate varies from 110 to 160 beats per minute. Active outdoor cats have slower heart rates than indoor sedentary cats. Kittens have rates of up to 260 beats per minute. Calculate and record your cat's normal resting heart rate.

The heart rate increases rapidly with excitement and exercise. It also increases when a cat is in pain, has a fever, is in the early stages of shock, has been frightened, poisoned, bitten, suffered an electric shock or has an overactive thyroid gland or heart disease. Calculate your cat's resting heart rate when it is fit and healthy.

1. Grasp the chest just behind the elbows. Feel for the heart, count beats for twenty seconds and multiply by three for the rate per minute.

Fig. 1: Feeling the heartbeat

Gently squeeze the chest behind the elbows to feel for and then count the heart rate. The heartbeat is easy to find in lean cats but more difficult to locate in fat ones. While feeling the heartbeat, support and control the cat with your other hand. Squeeze with about the same pressure you would use when squeezing a loaf of bread to check its freshness.

2. Monitor the pulse by placing your fingers inside the hind leg where it joins the body. Move them around until you feel the pulse then count for twenty seconds and multiply by three for the rate per minute.

Fig. 2: Finding the pulse

Press your fingertips into the slight groove in the leg. Feel for the pulse. If you apply too much pressure you will not be able to feel the pulse. It can be difficult to find the pulse even in a slim cat and very difficult in overweight cats.

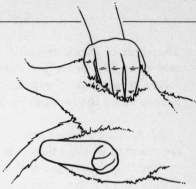

EXAMINING THE GUMS

The color of the gums is an important indicator of a cat's health. Pale or white gums can indicate shock. Cats with unpigmented 'nose buttons' show a pink colour similar to their gums. Unpigmented noses act as a reliable indicator of color, like rosy cheeks in healthy humans. Shock is the most serious emergency and takes precedence over other injuries. Even apparently mild trauma can lead to shock.

1. Examine the cat's gums by gently lifting the upper lip to expose the gums. Normal gums are a healthy pink color.

Fig. 1: Examine the gums

If the gums are pink, press your finger against them. If blood does not rush back in immediately, shock might be impending.

SHOCK

The signs of shock are: pale or white gums, a rapid heart rate over 250 beats per minute and fast breathing over forty breaths per minute. Whatever the emergency, always be on the lookout for signs of shock.

By checking a cat's heart rate, breathing rate and gums you are checking whether the cat is in shock. Shock can be caused by bleeding, burns, heart failure, vomiting and/or diarrhea, electrocution, severe trauma, insect and animal bites, diabetes, poisons and many other injuries, illnesses and accidents. Treating shock takes precedence over treating most other injuries, including fractures and broken bones. Untreated shock may lead to loss of consciousness and death.

The signs of early shock are:

- Faster than normal breathing
- Faster than normal resting heart rate
- Pale or light pink gums
- Restlessness or anxiety
- Lethargy or weakness
- Slow capillary refill time — more than two seconds
- Normal or just subnormal rectal temperature

The signs of late shock are:

- Shallow, slow breathing
- Irregular heartbeat
- Very pale or blue gums
- Lack of response
- Extreme weakness or unconsciousness
- Very slow capillary refill — more than four seconds
- Very cool body temperature — less than 36.7°C/98°F

Slow down the potentially catastrophic effects of shock by doing the following:

1. Place the cat on its side with head extended.
2. Elevate the hindquarters using pillows or towels.
3. Stop obvious bleeding using pressure or a tourniquet if necessary. (See page 23.)
4. Give artificial respiration or heart massage if necessary. (See page 13.)
5. Prevent loss of body heat by wrapping the cat in a warm blanket.
6. Transport to the nearest veterinarian immediately. If the cat is in deep shock, keep it cradled with limbs elevated above the heart.

- **Do not give anything to eat or drink**
- **Do not let a conscious cat wander about**

ANAPHYLACTIC SHOCK

Anaphylactic shock may be brought on by insect stings, drugs, or, very rarely, by food.

Recognizing anaphylactic shock:
- Has the cat just had an injection or been given medicines?
- Has it possibly been stung by an insect?
- Has it just eaten and is having difficulty breathing?
- Is the cat retching or vomiting?
- Does it have sudden diarrhea?
- Is the cat collapsing?
- Are the gums blue?
- Is the cat showing signs of shock?

1. Keep the airway open.
2. Give artificial respiration and heart massage if necessary. (See page 13.)

3. If the cat's lungs fill with liquid, it will start to make gurgling sounds while trying to breathe. Suspend the cat for ten seconds by its hind legs to try to clear the airway.
4. Get immediate veterinary assistance. (Urgent treatment is essential. The veterinarian will give drugs to stop the allergic swelling in the air passages.)

A less urgent allergic reaction to bites and injections causes the face to swell and become itchy. Sometimes the site of the bite or injection is itchy or hot and painful. Prevent your cat from mutilating itself by using an Elizabethan collar (see page 24) and monitor its reaction. Allergic reactions can suddenly develop into life threatening anaphylactic shock.

WHEN TO GIVE ARTIFICIAL RESPIRATION AND HEART MASSAGE

If a cat's brain does not receive oxygen for several minutes because either the heart or breathing has stopped, permanent brain damage results. This is one of the very few circumstances when the immediate provision of first aid may be life saving. When heart massage is combined with artificial respiration, the joint procedure is called cardiopulmonary resuscitation, or CPR. The abbreviation CPR is used throughout this book.

Assess the situation:

Causes of unconsciousness that may require CPR include: **Choking, Electrocution, Near-drowning, Smoke inhalation, Poisoning, Blood loss, Concussion, Fainting, Shock, Diabetes** and **Heart arrythmias and insufficiencies.**

(Strokes and heart attacks, the most common reasons for giving artificial respiration and heart massage to humans, are both uncommon in cats.)

ARTIFICIAL RESPIRATION AND HEART MASSAGE

Assess the cat's consciousness:

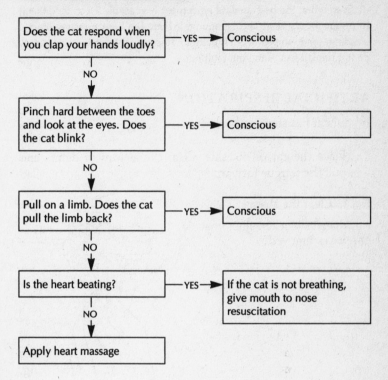

Does the cat respond when you clap your hands loudly? —YES→ Conscious

NO ↓

Pinch hard between the toes and look at the eyes. Does the cat blink? —YES→ Conscious

NO ↓

Pull on a limb. Does the cat pull the limb back? —YES→ Conscious

NO ↓

Is the heart beating? —YES→ If the cat is not breathing, give mouth to nose resuscitation

NO ↓

Apply heart massage

HOW TO GIVE CARDIOPULMONARY RESUSCITATION (CPR)

Artificial respiration (mouth to nose) and heart massage are two life saving procedures often called cardiopulmonary resuscitation or CPR. If your cat is not breathing and has no heartbeat, give CPR. To be effective, heart massage must be administered rhythmically with mouth to nose respiration.

Do not attempt either procedure unless it is obvious

13

that the cat is unconscious and will die without your help.

(Even when the best medical equipment is available it can be difficult to restart a cat's heart and breathing. If there has been massive internal bleeding, for example, it is virtually impossible. If you are unsuccessful, do not think it has been your fault.)

ARTIFICIAL RESPIRATION

If your cat has stopped breathing:

1. Place the cat on its side. Clear the airway of debris and pull the tongue forward.

Fig. 1: Clear the airway

Any material blocking the throat or nose is removed.

2. Close the cat's mouth. With your hand around the muzzle place your mouth over the cat's nose and blow in until you see the chest expand.

Fig. 2: Breathe into the cat's lungs

Your hand on the muzzle creates an airtight seal.

14

3. Take your mouth away and let the lungs deflate.
4. Repeat this procedure twenty to thirty times per minute.
5. Check the pulse every ten seconds to ensure the heart is still beating.
6. If the heart is not beating, give heart massage in conjunction with artificial respiration.
7. Get professional veterinary attention as soon as possible.

HEART MASSAGE

Feel for a heartbeat or pulse. Squeeze the gums and see if the squeezed area refills with blood when you remove your finger. If the cat's heart has stopped:

1. Place the cat on its side with the head lower than the body if possible. Grasp the chest between your thumb and fingers just behind the elbows. Place your other hand on the cat's back.

Fig. 1: Heart massage

The thumb and fingers of one hand squeeze together, compressing the ribs while the other hand supports the body. (Take care, when ribs are already broken, that they do not puncture the heart.)

2. Squeeze firmly, compressing the chest walls, squeezing up towards the neck. Be vigorous but not harsh. Do not worry about injuring or bruising the cat, this is a matter of life and death.

ARTIFICIAL RESPIRATION AND HEART MASSAGE

3. Repeat this pumping action one hundred times a minute using quick, firm pumps.
4. Apply heart massage for fifteen seconds, then mouth to nose respiration for ten seconds.
5. Check for a pulse. Continue heart massage until the pulse returns, then concentrate wholly on artificial respiration.
6. Get veterinary attention as soon as possible.

CPR by one person:
- Massage the heart for fifteen seconds
- Give mouth to nose respiration for ten seconds
- Continue until the heartbeat and breathing resumes
- Keep the cat warm and get veterinary help immediately

CPR by two people:
- One person applies heart massage for ten seconds then stops
- The second person gives two breaths into the cat's nose
- Continue these procedures rhythmically
- When the heart starts, continue artificial respiration
- The heart massager arranges transportation to the veterinarian while artificial respiration continues

CPR by three or more people:
- One person applies heart massage, the second artificial respiration and the third applies pressure in the groin.

(Elevating the hindquarters and applying pressure to the groin directs more blood to the brain where it is needed most.)

Fig. 4: Pressure in the groin

The hindquarters are raised and pressure applied to the groin to divert as much blood as possible to the brain.

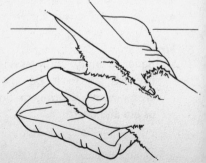

HOW TO CLEAN WOUNDS

When examining your cat you may come across an injury that needs your attention. Injuries are often painful. Take care to cause as little discomfort as possible, as even the gentlest cat may bite and scratch when frightened or in pain. Practice first aid when your cat is relaxed, fit and healthy by examining for wounds and then cleaning a designated area as you would if there were a genuine injury.

The two most common types of wounds are **closed**, where the skin is not broken, and **open**, where the skin is broken. **Fractures** can accompany either type of injury. With most wounds there is the danger of infection.

CLOSED WOUNDS

Closed wounds can be deceptive. Because the skin is not broken it looks like there is little damage. Do not underestimate a closed wound, it may look insignificant but underneath there can be dramatic internal injuries, the full extent of which may not be apparent for days. Even when wounds look minor, telephone your veterinarian and get professional advice.

The signs of closed wounds are:

- Swelling
- Pain
- Discoloration caused by bruising under the skin
- Increased heat in a specific location
- Superficial damage such as scratches to the skin

First aid for closed wounds:

1. Apply a cool compress to the wound as soon as possible after the injury. (A bag of frozen peas makes an ideal compress because it thaws faster than ice and molds to the contour of the injured area.)

Fig. 1: Apply an ice pack

Using a bag of frozen
vegetables, a towel soaked in
cold water or ice wrapped in a
towel, apply the cool compress
to the injured area.

2. If there is superficial skin damage such as scratching, clean
    with salt water (1 teaspoon salt to half a pint of water) or
    3% hydrogen peroxide.
3. Look for other hidden injuries, especially if your cat has
    been hit by a car. Contact your veterinarian for further
    advice.

OPEN WOUNDS

When the skin has been broken, underlying tissue is exposed
to dirt and bacteria. There is a great risk that these wounds
will become infected. Give immediate first aid to stop bleeding,
minimize further damage and control pain, then see your
veterinarian as soon as possible. Remember, although open
wounds may appear more serious, internal damage under
closed wounds can be equally life threatening.

The signs of open wounds are:

● Broken skin, sometimes only a puncture
● Pain
● Bleeding
● Increased licking or attention to a specific area

First aid for open wounds:
Wounds bleeding severely
1. Stop the bleeding by applying pressure. If first aid material is available use a non-stick pad, otherwise use any clean, absorbing material such as kitchen towel or a tea cloth. Do not remove the blood-soaked absorbing material. This disturbs the clot that has formed and bleeding may recur. Do not use disinfectants or antiseptics.

Fig. 1: Apply direct pressure to the bleeding wound

Press an absorbent pad held in your hand directly on the wound for two minutes. This allows a clot to form.

2. Add more absorbing padding if necessary and when possible elevate the injury above the cat's heart. **Do not elevate a leg if there is a possible fracture.**
3. Treat for shock (see page 10).

Detailed instructions on how to control bleeding on different parts of the body, how to find pressure points and how to apply a tourniquet are given under the heading **Bleeding** on page 71.

WOUNDS NOT BLEEDING SEVERELY

1. Flush minor wounds with 3% hydrogen peroxide, salt water or clean bottled or tap water.

2. Remove obvious dirt, gravel, splinters or other material from the wound, using tweezers or clean fingers. Clean the skin and hair around the wound with soap and water. Do not pull large objects like arrows or pieces of wood or metal out of open wounds — uncontrollable bleeding could follow. Go directly to the nearest veterinarian. (A water pik is ideal for cleaning wounds. Alternatively, use a clean hand-held garden spray water bottle with the nozzle turned to 'jet' rather than 'mist'.)

3. If hair is getting in the wound, cut it when it is damp for easy removal. Alternatively, lubricate the scissors with a small amount of petroleum jelly so that cut hair adheres to them or apply K-Y (water soluble) jelly to the wound, before clipping. Do not apply petroleum jelly to the wound. It is not water soluble and is difficult to remove later.

4. When the wound is cleaned and superficially disinfected, dab it dry with a clean cloth. Do not rub open wounds, you may cause more damage.

Do not underestimate small open wounds, injuries may be deep and severe. Be aware of the risk of infection. After giving immediate first aid always see your veterinarian as soon as possible.

ABSCESSES

Cats often suffer from bite abscesses from fights with other cats. The affected cat is irritable, 'growly' or acts like a tom cat immediately after a fight.

Look for tiny matts of clumped, dried hair. These matts form over the sites of puncture wounds. Get veterinary attention within twenty-four hours.

For more details on how to treat specific wounds see **Fishhooks** on page 111, **Puncture wounds** where cat fight abscesses are covered, on page 147 and **Bones** on page 78.

HOW TO APPLY BANDAGES

Bandages keep wounds dry and protect them from further injuries, including self-inflicted damage caused by biting, chewing and excessive licking. They also prevent injuries from becoming more contaminated and absorb seeping fluids. Bandaging provides constant mild pressure to control pain or bleeding. However, fully conscious cats are virtually impossible to bandage, as they resent being bandaged intensely. If bandages are needed, seek professional help.

For information, rather than practical purposes, these first aid techniques apply to bandaging.

GENERAL BANDAGE TECHNIQUE

1. After cleaning, disinfecting and drying a wound, place an absorbent pad over the affected area.
2. Starting over one edge of the pad, wrap gauze around so that the pad does not slip from its designated area.
3. Hold the end of the gauze with one hand to prevent it unravelling and apply the first wrap of adhesive tape at that point. Continue wrapping but extend the adhesive tape beyond the gauze at both ends of the bandage, catching bits of hair at these places. This helps to secure the bandage and prevents it from shifting. Do not use elastic bands on bandages, they can cut off circulation and cause overwhelming injuries.
4. Keep the bandage clean and dry. Cover it if necessary when your cat uses its litter tray. Do not let a bandage get wet.
5. Do not leave a bandage on for any excessive period of time. To do so increases the risk of infection or tissue death from poor circulation.
6. Bandaged wounds are highly susceptible to infection. If a wound becomes swollen or discharges pus, go to your vet. Remove bandages and get immediate veterinary

attention if there is an unpleasant smell coming from the wound.

7. Keep your cat indoors until healing has been completed and the bandage removed. Do not play active games with your cat while a wound is bandaged.

8. If your cat licks and pulls at its bandage your veterinarian can provide a plastic Elizabethan collar to be worn until the bandage is removed. Do not let your cat try to remove a bandage. See page 24 for how to make an emergency Elizabethan collar.

HOW TO MAKE A SPLINT

It is virtually impossible to apply a splint successfully to the limb of an unsedated cat. The cat contorts itself as it tries to avoid the splint, which causes more trauma than there might otherwise have been if you had left it alone. Do not try to apply a splint to a cat. To immobilize a dangling limb pull a small T-shirt over the cat, wrapping the whole trunk and affected limb together. Tights or panty hose can be used as an effective stockinette.

To splint a front leg:
1. Cut off both ends of one leg from a pair of tights and pull the leg over the cat's body.
2. Tape the ends of this stockinette to the cat's body and cut a hole for the uninjured leg to come through.

Fig. 1: Splinting a front leg with a stockinette made from a pair of tights

To splint a hind leg:
1.   Cut off a leg from a pair of tights and pull it over the cat's rump. Tape the cut end of the stockinette to the cat's chest.
2.   Cut a hole for the uninjured leg to come through.

If bone is visible, apply a clean pad over it before splinting. Do not put any ointment on this pad.

After any traumatic injury, always look for shock. Shock is life threatening. Treating shock takes precedence over splinting bones.

HOW TO APPLY A TOURNIQUET

Tourniquets are dangerous and can do more harm than good. Cats are unlikely to bleed to death from torn blood vessels on their limbs. Instead of a tourniquet, use pressure to stop bleeding. For suspected poisonous snake bites, use ice packs and immobilization rather than a tourniquet to control the spread of poison around the body. Apply a tourniquet only when bleeding from a leg is devastating and you cannot stop it by any other means. Do not practice applying a tourniquet to your cat, to do so would be painful and unpleasant.

1.   Wrap a piece of fabric (a tie, soft belt, torn sheet or gauze) above the bleeding wound and tie a knot.

Fig. 1: Tie a tight knot and insert a pencil into the wrapped material

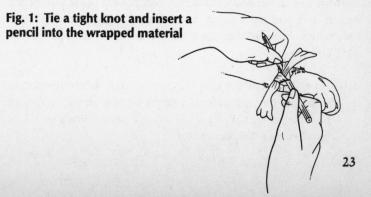

2. Slip a pen, pencil, stick, or other firm and slender material into the wrapped material and twist it until the bleeding stops.
3. Tie down the pencil with another piece of material, keeping the bandage firm and tight. Get immediate veterinary help.

Fig. 2: Tie the tourniquet in place

A tight tourniquet cuts off the blood supply. If it is left on too long it could lead to the 'death' of the limb.

HOW TO MAKE AN ELIZABETHAN COLLAR

Occasionally, it will be necessary for you to prevent your cat from licking or chewing itself, or pawing at and rubbing its face after an injury and before you can get to your veterinarian. Emergency Elizabethan collars can be made by cutting the bottom out of an appropriately sized plastic plant pot or ice cream tub, or by rolling up a fan-shaped piece of hard cardboard. The Elizabethan collar is secured by tape to the cat's collar.

1. Cut out the bottom of a plastic plant pot. Make four holes in the pot and slip pieces of gauze through them. Make sure the cut edges are not jagged and will not injure the cat's neck. Line the cut edges with adhesive tape.

2. Alternatively, cut a piece of cardboard in a fan shape then roll it up and tape or tie it together in a cone.

Fig. 1: Preparing an Elizabethan collar from a plant pot

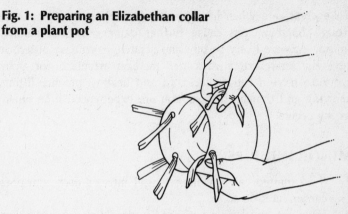

3. Make sure the cat is wearing a collar. If not, create a makeshift collar with a piece of gauze tied loosely around the neck. Slip the plant pot over the cat's head and tie it with the four tapes to the cat's collar.

Fig. 2: Secure the Elizabethan collar to the cat

Make sure it is not too tight. The collar should be large enough to fit just over the cat's head.

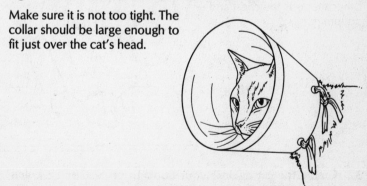

4. Keep the Elizabethan collar on the cat until you see your veterinarian.

HOW TO LIFT, CARRY AND TRANSPORT A CAT

Take great care when lifting and transporting an injured cat. Rough handling can cause further damage and is painful. Injured cats are likely to bite and scratch. If you are bitten or severely scratched, always get medical attention for your wounds. If your cat is placid, fit and healthy, practice lifting, carrying and transporting so you are experienced if an emergency occurs.

MINOR INJURIES

1. If an injured cat is willing to get into its own transport carrier, let it do so.
2. Lift a cat by placing one hand under its neck while using your other hand to support the back and body.

Fig. 1: Lifting a cat

One hand controls and supports the neck, preventing the cat from turning and biting. The other supports the chest and abdomen.

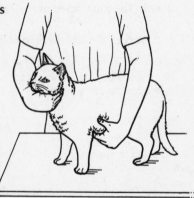

3. Cradle the cat against your body to protect its back and with your hand under the chest, lift it up and place it in the transport box. Put a blanket or towel in the transport box to provide cushioned support.

CRITICAL INJURIES

Critical injuries include all those that prevent the cat from moving itself and obvious serious injuries such as fractures or paralysis. Take extreme care when lifting a cat with potentially serious physical injuries:

- Support the back
- Keep broken legs up
- Keep injured chests down with the best lung up. (If the chest is injured and legs broken, the injured chest takes priority)
- Let the cat find its own comfortable breathing position

1. Keep the injured cat's back towards you.
2. Slide the cat on to a small board. (A large piece of corrugated cardboard offers good support.)

Fig. 2: A makeshift stretcher

Slip one hand under the cat's chest and the other under its rump. Gently pull it on to the stretcher.

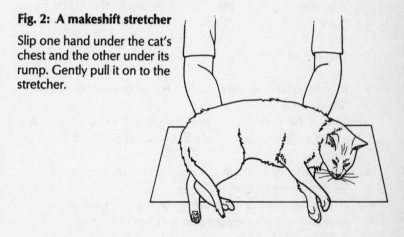

3. If additional help is not available always place the injured cat in a box for transportation. Cover it to prevent movement and conserve heat.
4. If a board is not available slide the cat on to a blanket or large towel. Wrap the blanket round the cat and use this for support.

Fig. 3: A blanket stretcher

Supporting both the front and rear of the body, the cat is lifted and pulled on to the folded blanket. Lift the cat by grasping the blanket as close to the body as possible.

5. Put a cat in a box or use the wrapped blanket for support while carrying it to the car.
6. Restrain the cat during transportation. If a box is not available and someone cannot sit with the injured cat, wrap it firmly in a blanket to conserve heat and reduce the risk of shock. (In cold weather turn on your car heater to keep the cat warm.)

- **If injuries are serious, do not waste time looking for items of support.**
- **Get to the veterinary clinic as quickly as possible but avoid sudden movements that may cause further injuries.**
- **When lifting and transporting an injured cat, avoid bending or twisting its body.**
- **If you must wrap a cat up for transportation, make sure there is no pressure on its chest and it can breathe freely.**

PART TWO

WHAT TO DO NEXT

Deciding If and When Your Cat Needs Veterinary Attention

Deciding whether your cat needs veterinary attention and, if so, when, can be difficult. For each emergency in this book there is a decision chart to help you decide what to do after you have provided first aid.

If your cat's life is in danger, if there is a risk of permanent injury or if your cat's problem causes obvious or hidden pain, the decision chart instructs you:

See a vet NOW

This means as soon as possible. Telephone ahead to make sure a veterinarian is available and get the cat to the clinic as soon as safety allows.

Other problems, although not as urgent, still require immediate veterinary treatment. For these conditions the decision chart indicates:

See a vet same day

For some conditions an appointment can wait until the next morning, but still make that telephone call as soon as possible.

There are other emergencies that need less urgent, follow-up veterinary treatment. The decision chart indicates:

See a vet within 24 hours

In these circumstances an appointment can wait until the next day.

Many conditions are neither life threatening nor cause pain, but with veterinary treatment the cat's life can be made more comfortable or prolonged. In these situations the decision chart indicates:

See a vet soon

The appointment can wait until a time convenient for both you and your veterinarian.

Many emergencies can be handled at home without the need for professional treatment. Although the chances of complications arising are small, hidden problems are possible and these may vary depending on where you live, the season of the year, and the age, size, sex or even breed of your cat. In these circumstances the decision chart indicates:

Phone for advice

Many incidents can be diagnosed and treated at home. Follow the instructions carefully. If your cat is not improving rapidly, even with your good care, contact your veterinarian.

Further Examination

WHEN, WHY AND HOW TO CARRY OUT A HEAD-TO-TAIL EXAMINATION

Once you have given life saving first aid, or after you have examined the cat and found its life not to be in imminent danger, it is important to carry out a further examination, looking for less obvious but potentially serious, painful or distressing conditions. While your cat is fit and healthy carry out the following procedures:

- Observe behavior and responses
- Listen to sounds
- Watch activities and movement
- Smell odors
- Take the temperature
- Examine the eyes, ears, nose and mouth
- Examine the head and neck
- Examine the body and limbs
- Examine the tail and anus
- Examine the skin and coat
- Observe gastrointestinal changes
- Monitor toilet habits
- Monitor eating and drinking changes
- Observe weight changes

Make your practice examination as simple as possible. Do not try to do everything in one session, your cat will get bored and try to leave. Remember to reward your cat's obedience with food treats, words of praise and petting. Give a reward after each step.

In real emergencies you will often not have time to carry out a complete head-to-tail examination, but by knowing what to do you can choose which parts are most important to carry out.

HOW TO TAKE A CAT'S TEMPERATURE

A cat's normal temperature is between 38.1 and 39.2°C/100.5 and 102.5°F. Nervousness and exercise raise body temperature, as do excess heat and infections. Temperatures below normal are caused by exposure to cold weather but also by shock. Record your cat's normal resting temperature. (When possible use a digital thermometer. They are accurate and easy to read.)

1. If using a glass thermometer, shake it down, lubricate the tip with K-Y (water soluble) jelly and, using a slight rotating action, insert the thermometer about 2.5 cm (1 inch) into the cat's rectum.
2. Keep hold of the thermometer and the cat's tail, wait for ninety seconds then remove, wipe clean and read. Disinfect the thermometer after each use.

*   **Do not try to take a cat's temperature by mouth.**
*   **Do not take a cat's temperature if it deeply resents your attempt to do so.**

Fig. 1: Taking a cat's temperature

While someone restrains the cat's body, grasp the tail at the base, raise it and insert the thermometer in the anus. Wrap the cat in a towel if necessary.

TEMPERATURE RANGE

°C	°F	
41.1 +	106 +	= cool cat down and seek veterinary attention immediately
40.6	105	= seek veterinary attention same day
40	104	= fever
39.4	103	= fever
38.9	102	= normal
38.3	101	= normal
37.8	100	= normal, but could indicate mild hypothermia – phone your vet
37.2	99	= seek veterinary attention same day
36.7 –	98 –	= keep cat warm and seek veterinary attention immediately

BEHAVIOR AND RESPONSE

Any change from normal behavior is cause for concern, even attractive changes. If your cat is normally aloof but now wants to be with you or it remains in one position all day, be on the look out for possible problems. Do not assume that a purring cat is a healthy, contented cat. Unexpected purring may indicate pain or distress.

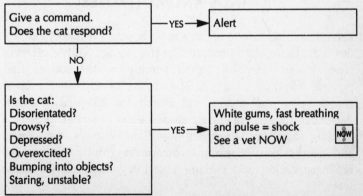

Give a command. Does the cat respond? — YES → Alert

NO

Is the cat: Disorientated? Drowsy? Depressed? Overexcited? Bumping into objects? Staring, unstable? — YES → White gums, fast breathing and pulse = shock See a vet NOW

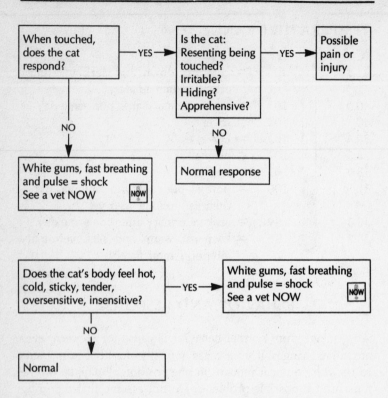

| When touched, does the cat respond? | —YES→ | Is the cat: Resenting being touched? Irritable? Hiding? Apprehensive? | —YES→ | Possible pain or injury |

NO ↓

White gums, fast breathing and pulse = shock See a vet NOW **NOW**

NO ↓

Normal response

Does the cat's body feel hot, cold, sticky, tender, oversensitive, insensitive? —YES→ White gums, fast breathing and pulse = shock See a vet NOW **NOW**

NO ↓

Normal

SOUNDS AND ACTIVITIES

Learn to recognize the unusual sounds your cat makes that are **not** a cause for alarm, sounds like the strange teeth chattering when it sees prey through a window or the sounds that precede vomiting a fur ball. Then listen for any other unusual sounds your cat makes and watch for changed routines. Abnormal sounds are almost always signs of serious problems needing same day veterinary attention. Changes in activities and routines usually warrant your carrying out a full head-to-tail examination and seeking veterinary attention the same week.

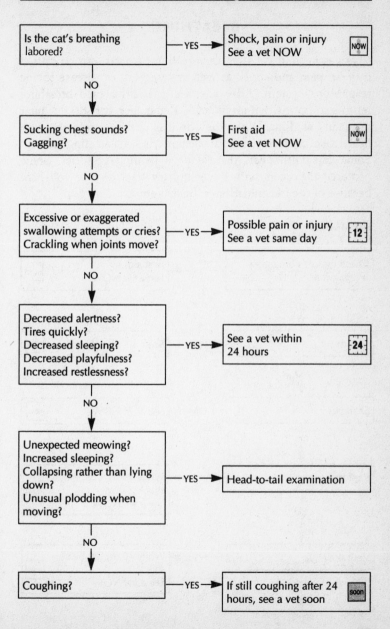

Is the cat's breathing labored? —YES→ Shock, pain or injury / See a vet NOW [NOW]

NO ↓

Sucking chest sounds? / Gagging? —YES→ First aid / See a vet NOW [NOW]

NO ↓

Excessive or exaggerated swallowing attempts or cries? / Crackling when joints move? —YES→ Possible pain or injury / See a vet same day [12]

NO ↓

Decreased alertness? / Tires quickly? / Decreased sleeping? / Decreased playfulness? / Increased restlessness? —YES→ See a vet within 24 hours [24]

NO ↓

Unexpected meowing? / Increased sleeping? / Collapsing rather than lying down? / Unusual plodding when moving? —YES→ Head-to-tail examination

NO ↓

Coughing? —YES→ If still coughing after 24 hours, see a vet soon [soon]

BREATHING

Changes in your cat's regular breathing pattern can be caused by fear, pain and shock as well as by injury or disease to the respiratory system. After exercise, a healthy cat's breathing returns to normal within minutes. Remember, cats do not pant as readily as dogs. When they do it is usually associated with heatstroke or, rarely, blood calcium crisis in lactating queens. Some cats with heart disease have panting episodes. Some neutered male cats with lower urinary tract disease will pant because of the inflammation to their urethra.

Breathing:

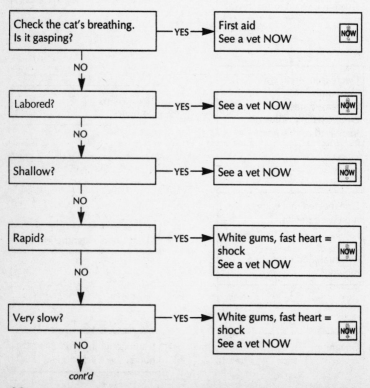

Check the cat's breathing. Is it gasping? —YES→ First aid / See a vet NOW

NO ↓

Labored? —YES→ See a vet NOW

NO ↓

Shallow? —YES→ See a vet NOW

NO ↓

Rapid? —YES→ White gums, fast heart = shock / See a vet NOW

NO ↓

Very slow? —YES→ White gums, fast heart = shock / See a vet NOW

NO ↓

cont'd

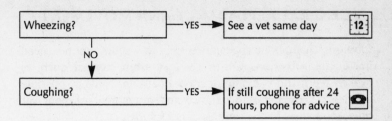

Wheezing? —YES→ See a vet same day **12**

NO ↓

Coughing? —YES→ If still coughing after 24 hours, phone for advice 📞

Panting:

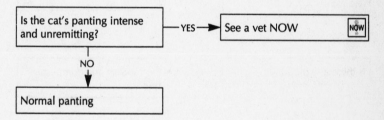

Is the cat's panting intense and unremitting? —YES→ See a vet NOW **NOW**

NO ↓

Normal panting

Related behavior:

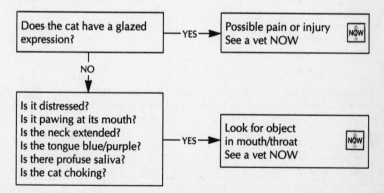

Does the cat have a glazed expression? —YES→ Possible pain or injury See a vet NOW **NOW**

NO ↓

Is it distressed?
Is it pawing at its mouth?
Is the neck extended?
Is the tongue blue/purple?
Is there profuse saliva?
Is the cat choking?
—YES→ Look for object in mouth/throat See a vet NOW **NOW**

GENERAL APPEARANCE AND MOVEMENT

Obvious changes in appearance such as visible wounds need immediate attention. Other changes from normal such as broken teeth and bleeding or frayed nails are signs of possible injuries. The general appearance and movement of your cat give good clues to the seriousness of injuries.

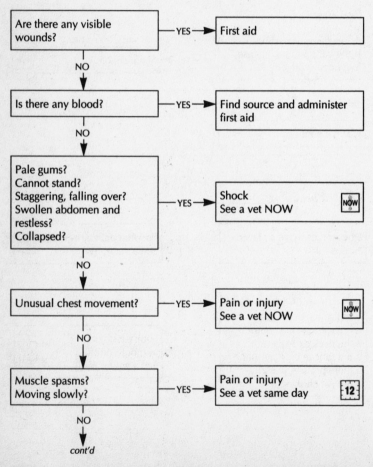

Are there any visible wounds? —YES→ First aid

NO ↓

Is there any blood? —YES→ Find source and administer first aid

NO ↓

Pale gums?
Cannot stand?
Staggering, falling over?
Swollen abdomen and restless?
Collapsed? —YES→ Shock
See a vet NOW **NOW**

NO ↓

Unusual chest movement? —YES→ Pain or injury
See a vet NOW **NOW**

NO ↓

Muscle spasms?
Moving slowly? —YES→ Pain or injury
See a vet same day **12**

NO ↓

cont'd

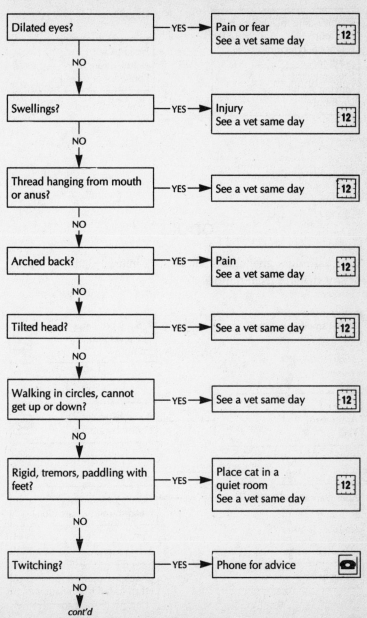

Dilated eyes? —YES→ Pain or fear
See a vet same day [12]

NO

Swellings? —YES→ Injury
See a vet same day [12]

NO

Thread hanging from mouth or anus? —YES→ See a vet same day [12]

NO

Arched back? —YES→ Pain
See a vet same day [12]

NO

Tilted head? —YES→ See a vet same day [12]

NO

Walking in circles, cannot get up or down? —YES→ See a vet same day [12]

NO

Rigid, tremors, paddling with feet? —YES→ Place cat in a quiet room
See a vet same day [12]

NO

Twitching? —YES→ Phone for advice

NO

cont'd

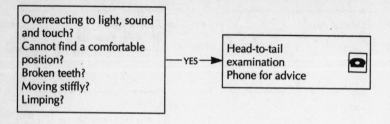

Overreacting to light, sound and touch?
Cannot find a comfortable position?
Broken teeth?
Moving stiffly?
Limping?

—YES→ Head-to-tail examination
Phone for advice

ODORS

Unusual odors give clues that a cat is injured or ill. Be aware of any changes from normal.

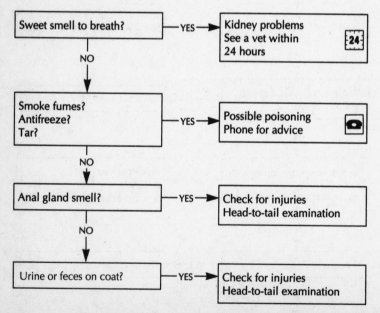

Sweet smell to breath? —YES→ Kidney problems
See a vet within
24 hours

NO ↓

Smoke fumes?
Antifreeze?
Tar? —YES→ Possible poisoning
Phone for advice

NO ↓

Anal gland smell? —YES→ Check for injuries
Head-to-tail examination

NO ↓

Urine or feces on coat? —YES→ Check for injuries
Head-to-tail examination

EXAMINE THE EYES, EARS, NOSE AND MOUTH

Eye injuries are common. Some are easily attended to at home while others that look only slightly different need professional attention. Give first aid for obvious injuries and protect the eyes from further damage. Bleeding from either the ears or nose after any trauma indicates that concussion is possible. Get veterinary attention as soon as possible. Other problems can often wait for twenty-four hours or be treated at home. A rapid check of the eyes, ears, nose and mouth reveals visible injuries but also tells you about the state of mind of the cat.

1. Check the eyes for discharge, clouding, redness, bleeding or injuries. Dilated pupils in good light mean fear, pain, excitement or shock or, in some instances, sudden blindness.
2. Test vision by flicking your finger at the eye. If your cat can see the finger it will blink.
3. Examine the ears for bleeding in the canals or external injuries. Flattened ears can mean pain, distress or weakness as well as anger.
4. Examine the nose for bleeding or discharge.
5. Check the mouth for foreign material or injuries to the tongue and hard palate. Internal mouth damage usually means there has been an injury at speed, for example a car accident or a fall.

Fig. 1: Examine the eyes

Check the eyes for abnormalities. Unusually dilated or wide eyes are cause for concern.

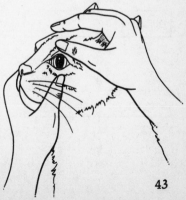

EYES

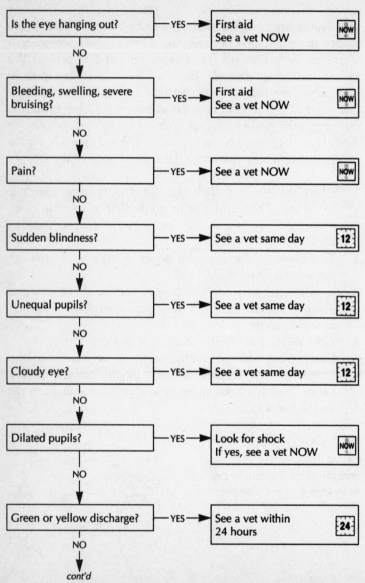

Is the eye hanging out?	—YES→	First aid See a vet NOW
↓ NO		
Bleeding, swelling, severe bruising?	—YES→	First aid See a vet NOW
↓ NO		
Pain?	—YES→	See a vet NOW
↓ NO		
Sudden blindness?	—YES→	See a vet same day
↓ NO		
Unequal pupils?	—YES→	See a vet same day
↓ NO		
Cloudy eye?	—YES→	See a vet same day
↓ NO		
Dilated pupils?	—YES→	Look for shock If yes, see a vet NOW
↓ NO		
Green or yellow discharge?	—YES→	See a vet within 24 hours
↓ NO		
cont'd		

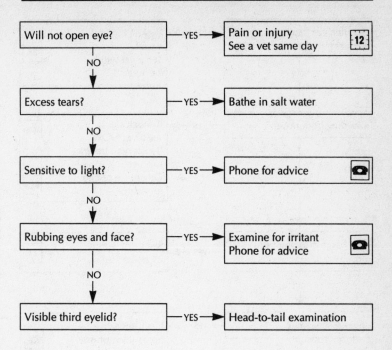

Will not open eye? — YES → Pain or injury
See a vet same day `12`

NO

Excess tears? — YES → Bathe in salt water

NO

Sensitive to light? — YES → Phone for advice `☎`

NO

Rubbing eyes and face? — YES → Examine for irritant
Phone for advice `☎`

NO

Visible third eyelid? — YES → Head-to-tail examination

EARS

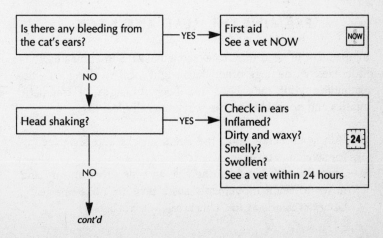

Is there any bleeding from the cat's ears? — YES → First aid
See a vet NOW `NOW`

NO

Head shaking? — YES → Check in ears
Inflamed?
Dirty and waxy?
Smelly?
Swollen?
See a vet within 24 hours `24`

NO

cont'd

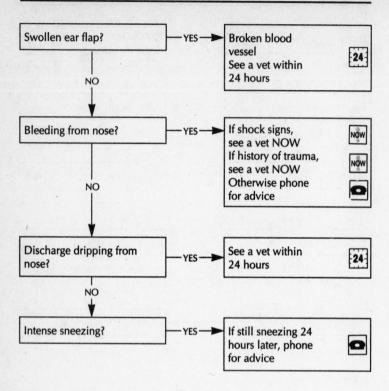

Swollen ear flap?	YES →	Broken blood vessel. See a vet within 24 hours
Bleeding from nose?	YES →	If shock signs, see a vet NOW. If history of trauma, see a vet NOW. Otherwise phone for advice
Discharge dripping from nose?	YES →	See a vet within 24 hours
Intense sneezing?	YES →	If still sneezing 24 hours later, phone for advice

EXAMINE THE HEAD AND NECK

Injuries to the head may cause concussion. Sometimes there is little external damage other than slight local swelling. Practice examining your cat's head and neck for signs of traumatic injuries and note what all the parts normally feel like.

1. Run your hands over the head, cheeks and jaws feeling for swellings or heat.
2. Turn the cat's head to one side and the other and up and down to see if movement causes pain. (In a true emergency, take extra care doing this. Cats in pain will lash out.)

3. Run your hands down the cat's neck, feeling under the hair for stickiness that might indicate a puncture wound, swelling or heat. (Air rifle injuries, for example, cause very small penetrations into which cats' hair is drawn.)

EXAMINE THE CHEST, ABDOMEN AND LIMBS

Body bruising is common after traffic accidents. Bites from cat fights and other penetrating wounds often do not bleed, but sticky or dried blood can be felt deep in the fur on the body, limbs or paws. Substantial swelling usually means that an abscess has formed. Car grease or tar means the cat has probably been hit by a vehicle. While your cat is relaxed and injury-free carry out a detailed physical feel of its body and limbs so that you know how it normally feels.

1. Run your hands firmly over the cat's back, chest and groin feeling for excess heat, stickiness or any sensitivity to touch.

Fig. 1: Examine the torso

With firm but not excessive pressure, feel all parts of the torso and especially around the bladder region for physical injuries or any sensitivity to touch. Take care over the ribs in case there are fractures.

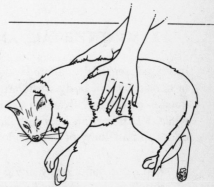

2. Part the hair and look for skin discoloration.
3. Run your hands down each leg. Examine both forelimbs and then hind limbs together, checking for symmetry.

4. Feel each joint and the paws for excess heat or swelling.
5. Examine the paws and claws for abrasions, tears, other injuries or traces of foreign material.

Understanding the lower urinary tract of cats is very important. Healthy cats are very secretive about their toilet habits. When life threatening disorders in urination occur the signs may be subtle or missed. Often they may be mistaken for constipation and treated for such at home, with tragic results.

1. Clean your cat's litter box frequently. Learn to recognize changes in volume of urine and frequency of urination.
2. If a change in urinary habits occurs, check the urine with a piece of white tissue for any change in colour. If there is a trace of pink, see your veterinarian within twenty-four hours.
3. Practice examining your cat's abdomen in the area of its urinary bladder. Ask your vet to rate your technique during your cat's annual examination. Once you are familiar with the normal feel you will readily be able to detect a blocked bladder.

EXAMINE THE TAIL, ANUS AND GENITALS

Increased sensitivity, altered odors or variation in the color or consistency of body waste are all clues to potential internal injuries or disease. Examine your cat's tail, anus and genitals while it is free from injury or illness to recognize the normal odors and anatomy of these regions.

1. Run your hand firmly along the length of the tail. There should be no obvious bumps or areas of excess heat. (The tail is a common site of bite injuries, especially near its base. Take care when making an examination, a cat in pain may lash out when touched.)

2. If a tail hangs limp, pinch it to see if the cat responds. (Lack of response means either a tail or spinal injury.)

3. Gently lift the cat's tail. The anal region should be clean with no signs of clinging waste. An intense and offensive smell means that the cat has emptied its anal glands. This is a clue that the cat has been frightened or injured.

4. Examine the scrotum for swelling or injuries, and the opening of the penis or vagina for inflammation or discharge.

5. Learn to recognize your cat's normal posture while urinating and defecating. Too often a life threatening urinary obstruction is wrongly diagnosed at home as just constipation' because the posture of a cat straining to relieve a urinary blockage is similar to when the cat empties its bowels.

If a normally tidy cat's coat smells of urine, this is a sign of either illness or injury.

SKIN AND COAT CONDITION

Skin problems seldom need immediate veterinary attention, and many can be controlled and eliminated without veterinary treatment. Others indicate that a cat has more serious internal problems.

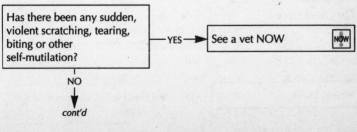

| Has there been any sudden, violent scratching, tearing, biting or other self-mutilation? | ——YES——▶ | See a vet NOW |

NO
▼
cont'd

SKIN AND COAT

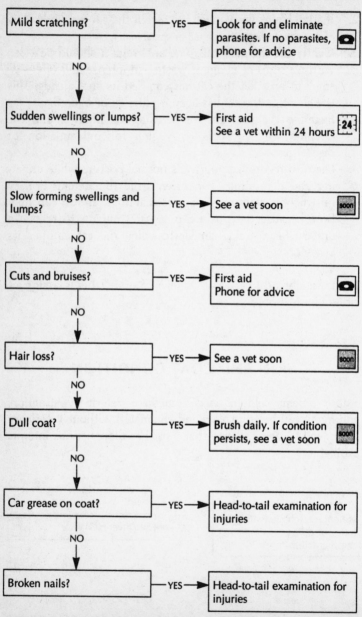

Mild scratching? —YES→ Look for and eliminate parasites. If no parasites, phone for advice 📞

NO ↓

Sudden swellings or lumps? —YES→ First aid
See a vet within 24 hours 24

NO ↓

Slow forming swellings and lumps? —YES→ See a vet soon [soon]

NO ↓

Cuts and bruises? —YES→ First aid
Phone for advice 📞

NO ↓

Hair loss? —YES→ See a vet soon [soon]

NO ↓

Dull coat? —YES→ Brush daily. If condition persists, see a vet soon [soon]

NO ↓

Car grease on coat? —YES→ Head-to-tail examination for injuries

NO ↓

Broken nails? —YES→ Head-to-tail examination for injuries

GASTROINTESTINAL CHANGES

Cats are usually quite particular about what they eat. Nevertheless hunger or curiosity take their toll on the gastrointestinal system. Some problems need the most urgent attention. Always err on the side of caution when deciding what to do.

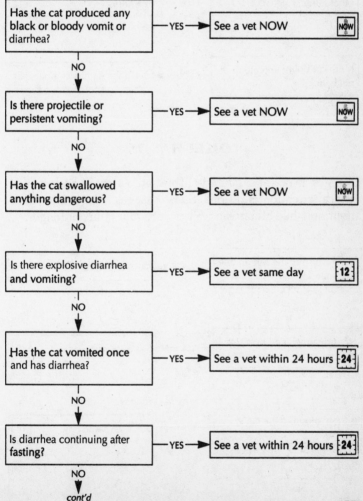

Has the cat produced any black or bloody vomit or diarrhea? —YES→ See a vet NOW

NO

Is there projectile or persistent vomiting? —YES→ See a vet NOW

NO

Has the cat swallowed anything dangerous? —YES→ See a vet NOW

NO

Is there explosive diarrhea and vomiting? —YES→ See a vet same day

NO

Has the cat vomited once and has diarrhea? —YES→ See a vet within 24 hours

NO

Is diarrhea continuing after fasting? —YES→ See a vet within 24 hours

NO

cont'd

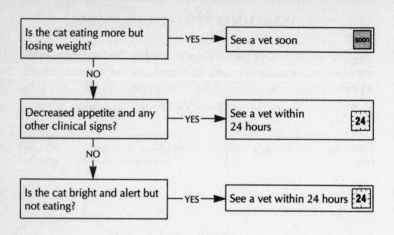

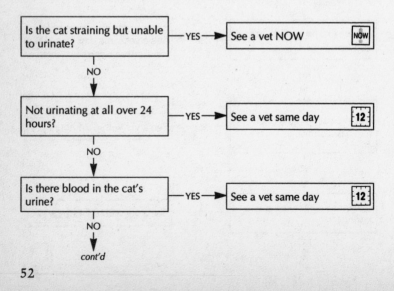

TOILET HABITS

Changes in a cat's sanitary habits are often indicators that medical attention is needed. Some changes require immediate attention while others can wait twenty-four hours or longer.

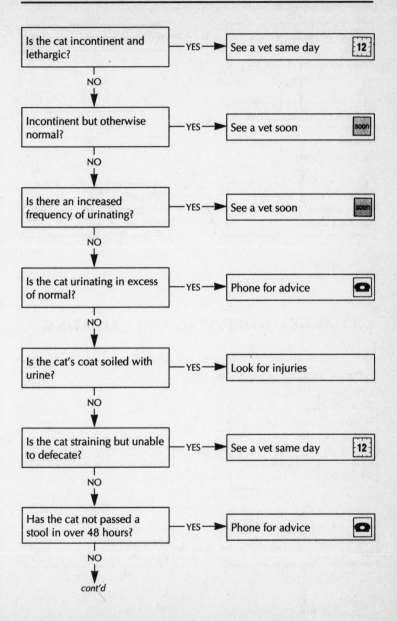

Is the cat incontinent and lethargic?	—YES→	See a vet same day **12**
↓ NO		
Incontinent but otherwise normal?	—YES→	See a vet soon **soon**
↓ NO		
Is there an increased frequency of urinating?	—YES→	See a vet soon **soon**
↓ NO		
Is the cat urinating in excess of normal?	—YES→	Phone for advice ☎
↓ NO		
Is the cat's coat soiled with urine?	—YES→	Look for injuries
↓ NO		
Is the cat straining but unable to defecate?	—YES→	See a vet same day **12**
↓ NO		
Has the cat not passed a stool in over 48 hours?	—YES→	Phone for advice ☎
↓ NO		

cont'd

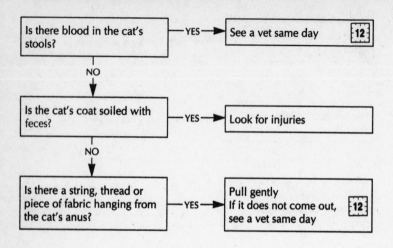

Is there blood in the cat's stools? —YES→ See a vet same day `12`

NO ↓

Is the cat's coat soiled with feces? —YES→ Look for injuries

NO ↓

Is there a string, thread or piece of fabric hanging from the cat's anus? —YES→ Pull gently. If it does not come out, see a vet same day `12`

CHANGES IN DRINKING AND URINATING

Increased thirst often indicates significant medical problems. Some of these need urgent attention.

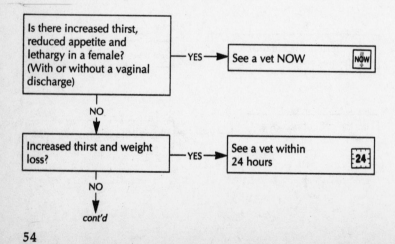

Is there increased thirst, reduced appetite and lethargy in a female? (With or without a vaginal discharge) —YES→ See a vet NOW `NOW`

NO ↓

Increased thirst and weight loss? —YES→ See a vet within 24 hours `24`

NO ↓

cont'd

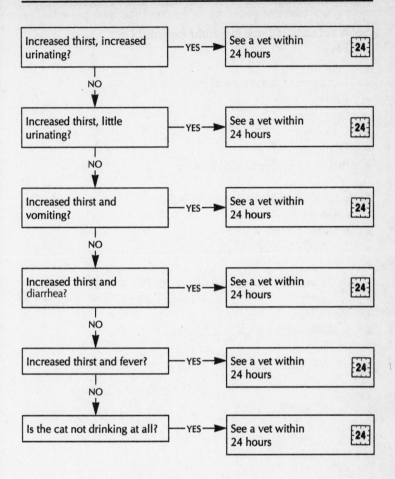

Increased thirst, increased urinating?	—YES→ See a vet within 24 hours
↓ NO	
Increased thirst, little urinating?	—YES→ See a vet within 24 hours
↓ NO	
Increased thirst and vomiting?	—YES→ See a vet within 24 hours
↓ NO	
Increased thirst and diarrhea?	—YES→ See a vet within 24 hours
↓ NO	
Increased thirst and fever?	—YES→ See a vet within 24 hours
↓ NO	
Is the cat not drinking at all?	—YES→ See a vet within 24 hours

WEIGHT CHANGES

An unexpected change in weight is a subtle sign that there are medical problems. Weight loss not related to any change in diet is worrying, although unexpected weight gain also can be a sign of disease.

55

See a vet soon if there is weight loss and:
- Fever
- Lethargy
- Increased or decreased appetite
- Restlessness
- Lameness
- Vomiting
- Diarrhea
- Increased or decreased drinking

See a vet soon if there is weight gain and:
- Lethargy
- Increased thirst
- Dull coat
- Hair loss
- Reduced appetite
- Shivering
- Vomiting
- Shaking

PART THREE

EMERGENCIES

Principles of First Aid

Follow these simple principles when faced with a feline emergency:

- **Do not panic**
  Stay calm. The cat's life may depend upon your common sense.
- **Assess the situation**
  What has happened?
- **Are you in danger?**
  Do not take foolish risks.
- **Is the cat in further danger?**
  Carefully move the cat if it is safe to do so.
- **Assess the cat's condition**
  Is it conscious or unconscious? Do not waste time with a detailed examination or diagnosis until immediate problems are treated.
- **Give emergency first aid**
  Give artificial respiration and heart massage if necessary.
- **Get help if necessary or available**
  When possible, one person organizes equipment and transport while the other tends to the injured cat.

- **Transport the cat to the vet**
- **Watch for shock**
  Regardless of its specific cause, shock is the most likely
  life threatening emergency you will encounter.

WATCH FOR SHOCK

Pale or white gums, rapid breathing, weak and rapid pulse, cold extremities, general weakness.

(For treatment of shock see under **Shock** on page 10.)

How to Use This Part

In this part emergencies are listed in alphabetical order. If your
cat is ill or injured, decide what the most important clinical
sign is: burns, eye injuries, poisons, scratching, etc., then look
under the appropriate heading. Alternatively, look in the index
at the end of the book to find the section you need.

This part describes most of the common emergencies you
will encounter. For each emergency there is a **description** of
the signs of the injury or illness and then **illustrated instructions** showing what to do.

Deciding whether your cat needs veterinary attention and,
if so, when, can be difficult. For each emergency there is a
decision chart to help you decide what to do after you have
provided first aid. For a full explanation of the symbols and
information in the decision charts, see under **Deciding If and
When Your Cat Needs Veterinary Attention** on page 31.

Immediate First Aid for the Conscious Cat

When emergencies happen, remember to assess the situation and the cat's condition. Do not get diverted by obvious injuries such as minor cuts and wounds. Restrain the cat when necessary, look for signs of shock, check the cat for any life threatening signs then carry out any necessary minor first aid.

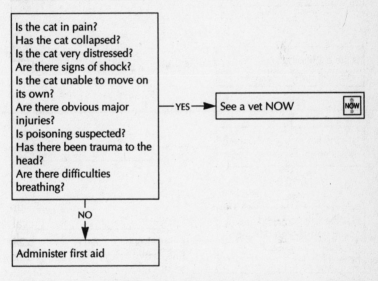

Is the cat in pain?
Has the cat collapsed?
Is the cat very distressed?
Are there signs of shock?
Is the cat unable to move on its own?
Are there obvious major injuries?
Is poisoning suspected?
Has there been trauma to the head?
Are there difficulties breathing?

── YES ──▶ See a vet NOW [NOW]

NO

Administer first aid

If there are potentially life threatening situations see your veterinarian immediately. Otherwise, provide first aid and follow the advice in the decision charts.

AGGRESSION AND BEHAVIOR CHANGES

Aggression is perfectly normal under many circumstances. However, aggression can also be a sign of illness or disease. Unexpected aggression from a normally placid and amenable cat can be caused by pain (especially from a blocked bladder), fever, brain damage (including tumours), infections (including rabies), head wounds, convulsions and seizures, diabetic crisis and panic attacks (especially after cat fights), that require veterinary attention. If your cat suddenly becomes aggressive, consider the following:

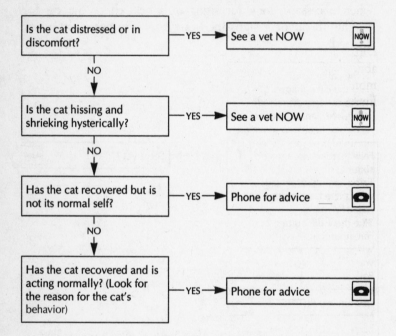

1. Protect yourself, other people and other animals from bites and scratches.
2. Reduce sensory stimulation by eliminating noise and light.
3. When your cat has become calmer, speak to it soothingly. If it permits you to do so, put it in a quiet room for several hours.
4. If the cat does not calm down, in the absence of the risk of rabies, throw a blanket over it, put it in a cat carrier

and take it to the vet. When rabies is a possible cause of the behavior change, telephone for professional assistance from your veterinarian or animal control agency (Dog Wardens, ASPCA or Police).

BIRTH

Difficulties at birth can be caused by weak contractions or abnormalities to the fetus. Older and overweight cats are more likely to suffer from weak contractions than others. Immature cats are more likely to abandon the new litter.

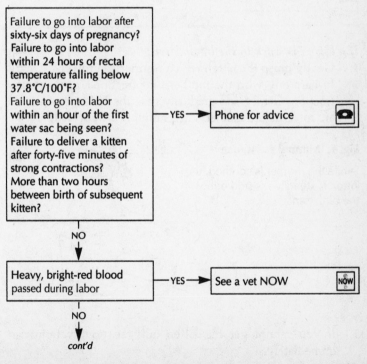

Failure to go into labor after sixty-six days of pregnancy?
Failure to go into labor within 24 hours of rectal temperature falling below 37.8°C/100°F?
Failure to go into labor within an hour of the first water sac being seen?
Failure to deliver a kitten after forty-five minutes of strong contractions?
More than two hours between birth of subsequent kitten?

— YES → Phone for advice

NO ↓

Heavy, bright-red blood passed during labor — YES → See a vet NOW

NO ↓

cont'd

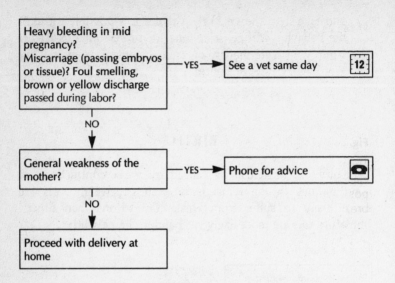

Heavy bleeding in mid pregnancy? Miscarriage (passing embryos or tissue)? Foul smelling, brown or yellow discharge passed during labor? —YES→ See a vet same day `12`

NO ↓

General weakness of the mother? —YES→ Phone for advice 📞

NO ↓

Proceed with delivery at home

If a kitten is stuck in the birth canal:

1. Gently grasp the kitten with a warm, clean towel.
2. In harmony with the mother's contractions, apply steady traction. Gently and gradually ease the kitten down in an arc towards the mother's heels until it is delivered.

Fig. 1: Manual assistance

While the mother is soothed, the kitten is steadily assisted out of the birth canal.

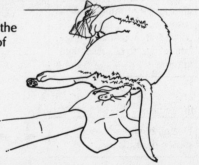

3. If you cannot get the kitten out, see your veterinarian immediately.

If the mother does not show interest in the kitten:

1. Place the newborn kitten on a warm, clean towel.
2. Using the towel, peel the membranes from around the kitten's head then off the body. The membranes will gather around the umbilical cord. (Do not pull on or cut the cord.)

Fig. 2: Remove the membranes

The mouth and nostrils are cleared of fluid making it possible for the kitten to breathe.

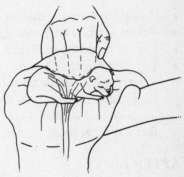

3. After wiping fluid from the kitten's face, rub its body with the towel vigorously to stimulate breathing.
4. If the kitten does not breathe, cradle it in the towel between your cupped hands. Raise your hands to shoulder height then swing them down rapidly in an arc to expel fluid from the air passages. Repeat this several times.

Fig. 3: Expel fluid from air passages

Hold the kitten firmly while swinging your cupped hands in an arc, then remove expelled fluid from the nose and mouth.

5. Rub the kitten vigorously with the towel. Stop treatment when it actively breathes, cries or moves.
6. Return the kitten to its mother. If she is unwilling to care for it, contact your veterinarian. (If the mother does not chew off the afterbirth, tie a thread round each umbilical cord about 2.5 cm (1 inch) from the kitten's abdomen. Cut off the afterbirth, leaving the tied thread on the portion attached to the kitten.)

- Avoid stressing the mother during normal birth
- Allow no visits from strangers
- Do not move the mother during any stage of normal birth
- Use a flashlight rather than bright lights for illumination
- Take care with umbilical cords, especially in the case of long-haired mother cats. A dried up cord can accidentally wrap around a kitten's limb and act as a tourniquet. Ensure that umbilical cords are severed.

AFTER BIRTH

Emergencies after birth are unlikely but can occur. Both the newborn kittens and the mother are susceptible to infection. The kittens also risk being abandoned if the mother is inexperienced or frightened. Very rarely the mother cat can tremble and stagger, suffering from low blood calcium. If left untreated this condition can be fatal.

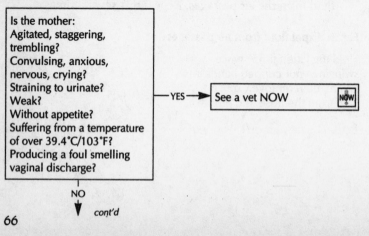

Is the mother:
Agitated, staggering, trembling?
Convulsing, anxious, nervous, crying?
Straining to urinate?
Weak?
Without appetite?
Suffering from a temperature of over 39.4°C/103°F?
Producing a foul smelling vaginal discharge?

→ YES → See a vet NOW

NO

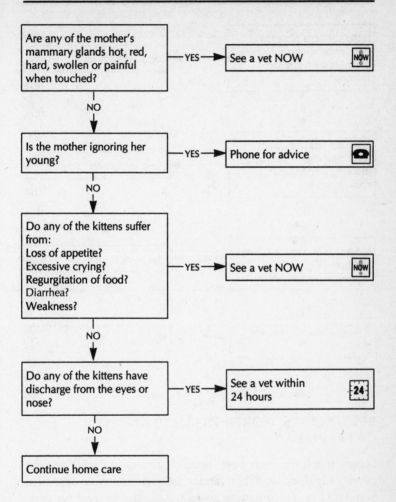

Are any of the mother's mammary glands hot, red, hard, swollen or painful when touched? —YES→ See a vet NOW | NOW

NO ↓

Is the mother ignoring her young? —YES→ Phone for advice

NO ↓

Do any of the kittens suffer from:
Loss of appetite?
Excessive crying?
Regurgitation of food?
Diarrhea?
Weakness? —YES→ See a vet NOW | NOW

NO ↓

Do any of the kittens have discharge from the eyes or nose? —YES→ See a vet within 24 hours | 24

NO ↓

Continue home care

BITES AND STINGS

Bites and stings often occur unseen. The cat returns home in distress or discomfort.

Animal bites are covered under **Puncture wounds** on page 146.

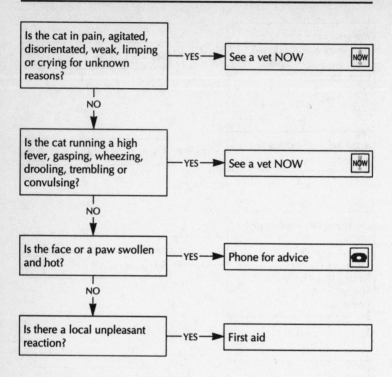

Is the cat in pain, agitated, disorientated, weak, limping or crying for unknown reasons? —YES→ See a vet NOW

NO ↓

Is the cat running a high fever, gasping, wheezing, drooling, trembling or convulsing? —YES→ See a vet NOW

NO ↓

Is the face or a paw swollen and hot? —YES→ Phone for advice

NO ↓

Is there a local unpleasant reaction? —YES→ First aid

BEES, WASPS, HORNETS, ANTS AND CATERPILLARS

Stings and bites from bees, wasps, hornets and ants usually cause only local irritation and relatively harmless reactions. Some cats suffer from more acute and life threatening systemic allergic reactions that need immediate veterinary treatment. Contact with some types of caterpillar causes intense local itching and irritation.

The signs of local reaction are: pain, itching and swelling in an area that has been stung, usually the mouth or paws.

The signs of more serious reaction are: difficulty breathing, shock, vomiting, diarrhea and coma.

First aid for local reactions:
1. When possible, remove embedded stingers with tweezers or by scraping the area with a credit card. (Do not squeeze the embedded stinger. This may release further irritant.)

Fig. 1: Remove the stinger

The cat is restrained and the stinger removed by scraping the skin with a credit card.

2. Apply a cold pack to the swollen area.
3. Give one half of a non-prescription antihistamine tablet.

First aid for severe reactions:
1. Get veterinary attention as quickly as possible. (The air passages may be swollen. It might be impossible to inflate the lungs with artificial respiration alone.)
2. Give CPR if the heart has stopped.
3. Give artificial respiration if breathing has stopped.
4. Treat for shock. (Severe reactions do not respond to first aid. Adrenalin and cortisone are necessary to reverse the allergic reaction.)

POISONOUS SNAKES, SPIDERS, SCORPIONS

Poisonous snakes (adders in the UK, rattlesnakes in Canada, copperheads and cottonmouths in the USA) bite cats far more frequently than they bite humans. It is unusual to see a cat actually being bitten.

The signs of a poisonous snakebite are: trembling, excitement, vomiting, collapse, drooling saliva, dilated pupils and fast pulse.

Poisonous spiders rarely bite cats because spiders' mouth parts can only pierce thin skin, like the skin between the toes. Bites are a potential worry only where poisonous spiders exist such as Australia and the USA.

The signs of a poisonous spider bite are: severe pain at the site of the bite (usually the paw), drooling, vomiting, convulsions, muscle spasms and breathing difficulties.

Scorpions sting inquisitive cats with the venom in the last segment of the tail. There is a hazard to cats in parts of Arizona and New Mexico.

The signs of a scorpion sting are: severe pain at the site of the bite (usually the paw), drooling, general weakness, breathing difficulties and paralysis.

First aid for snake, spider and scorpion bites:

1. Minimize the cat's movement. (Excess movement speeds the poison through the body.)
2. If the bite wound is visible, wash it thoroughly with cold water to get rid of any surface venom. (Do not cut the wound or attempt to suck out venom. This increases the blood supply and makes the condition worse.)
3. If a leg is bitten, keep it below the heart, apply an ice pack (a bag of frozen vegetables) and bandage it, wrapping large sheets of cotton wool tightly around the limb and covering this with firm elastic adhesive bandage. (Tourniquets are not as effective as bandages in slowing the spread of poison.)
4. Put the cat in a covered box and see a local veterinarian immediately. When given promptly, anti-venom and cortisone save lives.

POISONOUS TICKS

Some **ticks** in Australia, the USA and Canada produce a toxin that causes paralysis and death in cats. These ticks must be on their victim for two days to cause problems. Because cats are such excellent self-cleaners, tick transmitted diseases are uncommon in the species.

First aid for tick infestation:
1. Comb through the cat's fur with your fingertips.
2. Remove ticks by inverting a small container of alcohol or methylated spirit over the tick. This kills the tick. (Do not squeeze the tick. Squeezing may cause more poison to be injected into the cat.)
3. With tweezers, gently twist the mouth piece to remove the tick from the cat's skin.

BLEEDING

External bleeding is obvious, but **internal bleeding** – though less obvious – is equally important. If your cat has had a major injury or is acting in a subdued manner, look for signs of shock.

Spurting blood means an artery has been cut. It may be difficult to stop arterial bleeding but once the severed vessel is located, direct pressure can stop the bleeding immediately.

> ### WATCH FOR SHOCK
>
> **Pale or white gums, rapid breathing, weak and rapid pulse, cold extremities, general weakness.**
>
> (For treatment of shock see under **Shock** on page 10.)

Cleaning and bandaging wounds is covered on pages 17–22.

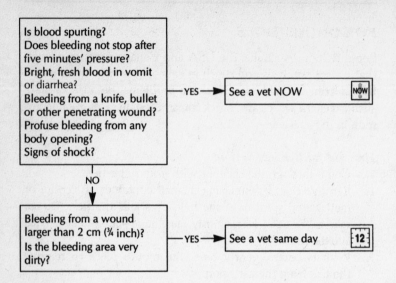

Is blood spurting?
Does bleeding not stop after five minutes' pressure?
Bright, fresh blood in vomit or diarrhea?
Bleeding from a knife, bullet or other penetrating wound?
Profuse bleeding from any body opening?
Signs of shock?

YES → See a vet NOW

NO ↓

Bleeding from a wound larger than 2 cm (¾ inch)?
Is the bleeding area very dirty?

YES → See a vet same day

INTERNAL BLEEDING

1. If the cat has collapsed, place it on its side with the head extended.
2. Elevate the hindquarters using a folded blanket, towel or pillow.

Fig. 1: Treat for shock

The hindquarters are elevated, a wrapped hot water bottle provides extra warmth and the cat is covered in blankets while it is taken as quickly as possible to the veterinarian.

3. Wrap the cat in coats or blankets and take to the veterinarian immediately.

BLEEDING FROM THE HEAD, MOUTH AND TORSO

1. Restrain the cat.
2. Clean minor wounds. Apply pressure immediately to more severe bleeding by covering the wound with an absorbent pad. Maintain pressure for two minutes. (Sanitary towels are excellent for covering bleeding wounds.)
3. Do not remove the absorbent pad. Hold it securely in place with gauze or torn sheets, wrapped just tightly enough to keep the pad on the wound. (Sometimes life threatening blood loss occurs from chronic ulcers on the roof of the mouth. The cat swallows most of the blood, making the problem difficult to detect. When this type of chronic blood loss occurs your cat might cry loudly, have dilated eyes, collapse or have epilepsy-like seizures. See your vet immediately.)

Fig. 2: Bleeding from the torso

The absorbent pad is held in place with gauze dressing wrapped just tight enough to keep it on the wound.

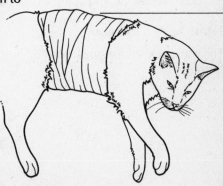

4. See your veterinarian immediately.

BLEEDING EAR

1. Apply pressure on both sides of the ear flap with absorbent pads for several minutes.

Fig. 3: Apply pressure to ear flap

The cat is restrained and
pressure is applied for several
minutes with an absorbent pad.

2. See your veterinarian the same day.

BLEEDING NOSE

1. Restrain the cat and apply a cold pack to the nose.

Fig. 4: Apply a cold pack

The cold pack reduces the blood
flow.

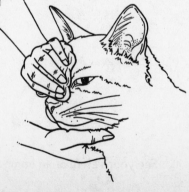

2. Help a clot to form by holding an absorbent pad over the nostril.

Fig. 5: Cover the nostril

3. Nosebleeds are caused by trauma or other damage in the nose. Telephone your veterinarian for advice.

BLEEDING LIMB

1. For minor bleeding, restrain the cat, apply pressure to the bleeding wound with an absorbent pad, clean with 3% hydrogen peroxide.
2. For serious bleeding, apply pressure at the following pressure points:

Fig. 6: Front leg

With your thumb on the outside, grasp the front leg halfway between the shoulder and elbow. Press firmly with the flat of your fingers to reduce bleeding.

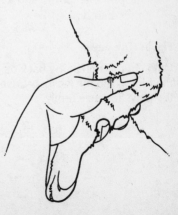

Fig. 7: Back leg

Grasp the leg as close to the
groin as possible and squeeze.
Alternatively, feel for the pulse
with your fingers then apply firm
pressure to stop blood flowing.

3. Elevate the leg above the heart.
4. Get veterinary attention immediately.

BLEEDING PAW

1. Restrain the cat and clean minor wounds with 3% hydro-
    gen peroxide. Look for and remove visible foreign objects
    such as pieces of glass. (Do not use antiseptics that sting.)
2. Using a clean absorbent pad, apply pressure. If blood
    seeps through, do not remove the pad, add more padding.
3. If bleeding continues after four minutes, apply pressure to
    the pressure point and take the cat to your veterinarian
    immediately.

Fig. 9: The paws

With your thumb at the back of
the foot, grasp the leg just above
the paw. Squeeze firmly.

4.   Alternatively, using a tie or torn piece of soft material, apply a tourniquet and take to your veterinarian immediately. (Do not leave a tight tourniquet on the paw for more than fifteen minutes. Loosen it for two minutes then tighten again only if absolutely necessary. Used wrongly, tourniquets can be extremely damaging.)

BLEEDING CLAW

1.   Restrain the cat and apply a clean absorbent pad to the bleeding claw.
2.   Only remove the broken nail if it is hanging so loose that it moves easily when you touch it. Give it a quick pull with your fingers.

Fig. 10: Broken claws

(a) This claw can be removed with a quick pull.

(b) Do not try to remove this claw. Get veterinary treatment to remove pain and control infection.

3.   If the claw is still partly attached, see your veterinarian within twenty-four hours. (If bleeding occurs while cutting your cat's claws because you cut one too short, apply pressure with a clean absorbent pad for two minutes.)

BLEEDING TAIL

1. With your thumb below and in the soft middle of the tail and your fingers above, apply pressure with your thumb to control bleeding.
2. If the tip of the tail is still bleeding, see a veterinarian within twenty-four hours.

BONES

Bones are most often damaged through injuries caused by traffic accidents and falls. If the bone breaks through the skin and is **open**, it can easily become infected. **Closed** fractures, where the bone does not break through, and dislocations, where a bone is pulled out of its socket, are just as dangerous and painful to the cat but not as readily apparent. If a fracture is closed one of your important objectives is to prevent it from becoming open.

Muscle, ligament and tendon injuries can cause clinical signs similar to those caused by broken bones. First aid for these conditions is covered under **Lameness** on page 122.

WATCH FOR SHOCK

Pale or white gums, rapid breathing, weak and rapid pulse, cold extremities, general weakness.

(For treatment of shock see under **Shock** on page 10.)

For all fractures, provide support to reduce pain and the risk of further injuries during transport. Do not try to reset fractures. Do not use antiseptics or any type of ointments on open fractures.

SPINAL FRACTURES

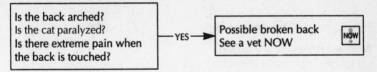

Is the back arched?
Is the cat paralyzed?
Is there extreme pain when
the back is touched?

— YES →

Possible broken back
See a vet NOW

1. Restrain with a towel around the neck if necessary.
2. Without bending the cat's back, gently pull the cat on to a flat board and strap it down, taking care to avoid pressure on the neck. (A piece of removable shelving works well but make sure it fits in your car.)

Fig. 1: Avoid manipulating the back

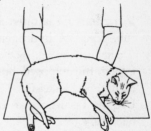

One hand is placed under the shoulders and the other under the hip bone. Slide the cat carefully on to firm transport. Sometimes 'scruffing' the cat causes it less agitation.

3. Take the cat to the veterinarian immediately. **Do not try to splint a broken back.**

LIMB FRACTURES

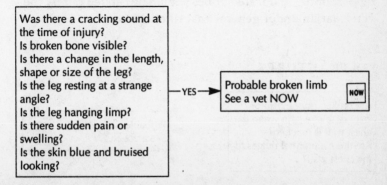

Was there a cracking sound at
the time of injury?
Is broken bone visible?
Is there a change in the length,
shape or size of the leg?
Is the leg resting at a strange
angle?
Is the leg hanging limp?
Is there sudden pain or
swelling?
Is the skin blue and bruised
looking?

— YES →

Probable broken limb
See a vet NOW

1. Restrain the cat if necessary.
2. Gently slide a clean towel under the limb.

Fig. 2: Support the broken leg

A folded towel, gently pulled under the broken leg provides support when the cat is moved.

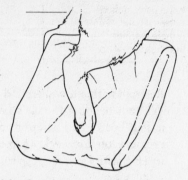

3. If the fracture is **open** and broken bone is visible, do not rub, pour 3% hydrogen peroxide over the open wound. (Do not use any antiseptic on the open wound.)
4. Cover the exposed bone with clean gauze. (Use medical bandage, a clean tea towel or a sanitary towel.)
5. Use a T-shirt as a tube bandage only if absolutely necessary.
6. Support the broken leg with the folded towel, keep the cat warm to prevent shock, lift the cat and take to the veterinarian immediately.

Do not try to reset broken bones. Resetting, including repositioning dislocated bones should be carried out by the veterinarian under general anaesthetic.

RIB FRACTURES

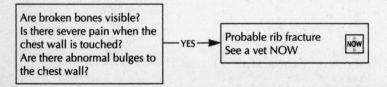

Are broken bones visible?
Is there severe pain when the chest wall is touched?
Are there abnormal bulges to the chest wall?

—YES→

Probable rib fracture
See a vet NOW

NOW

A sucking sound means the chest cavity has been penetrated.

1. Restrain the cat if necessary.
2. If there are open wounds, cover them with clean gauze.
3. Wrap torn sheets firmly around the chest but not so firm that they interfere with breathing. If you have a helper, have that person hold the palm of his or her hand over the sucking wound on the way to the veterinarian. The cat's own fat layer sometimes seals a chest wound. This is a rare instance where petroleum jelly on a pad may be applied to a wound to help make an airtight seal.

Fig. 4: Wrap the chest wall

Gauze bandage or torn sheet is wrapped around the chest wall to provide firm support.

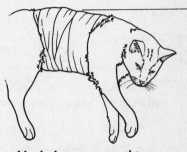

4. If part of the chest wall is softly bulging, wrap this area first, using enough pressure to eliminate the bulge. (A hard bulge is usually the broken end of a rib. A soft bulge means the lung is possibly punctured, deep muscles are damaged and air is trying to escape.)
5. Take the cat to the veterinarian immediately. (Do not pick up or support the cat by its chest.)

TAIL FRACTURES

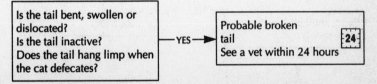

Is the tail bent, swollen or dislocated?
Is the tail inactive?
Does the tail hang limp when the cat defecates? ── YES ➔ Probable broken tail — See a vet within 24 hours — 24

1. Attempting to bandage a tail is almost pointless. Leave it alone.
2. Make an appointment to see your veterinarian during the next twenty-four hours.

BREATHING PROBLEMS

Although some breathing difficulties are minor, others can be life threatening. Remember, rapid or light breathing can mean shock.

WATCH FOR SHOCK

Pale or white gums, rapid breathing, weak and rapid pulse, cold extremities, general weakness.

(For treatment of shock see under **Shock** on page 10.)

Breathing problems can originate in the air passages themselves, but they can also be secondary to serious conditions in other parts of the body. Treat most breathing difficulties as potentially serious emergencies.

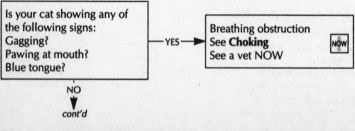

Is your cat showing any of the following signs:
Gagging?
Pawing at mouth?
Blue tongue?

—YES→ Breathing obstruction
See **Choking**
See a vet NOW

NO

↓

cont'd

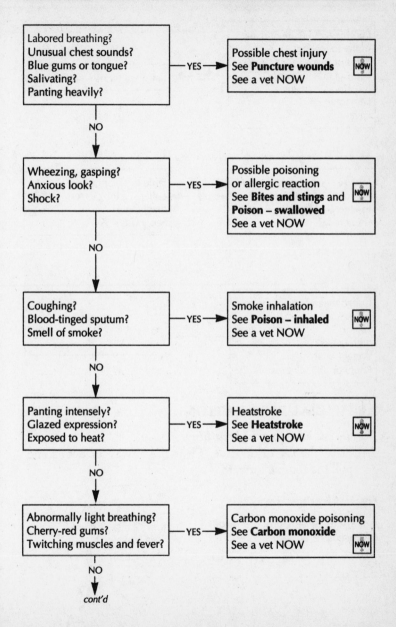

Labored breathing?
Unusual chest sounds?
Blue gums or tongue?
Salivating?
Panting heavily?
—YES→
Possible chest injury
See **Puncture wounds**
See a vet NOW

NO↓

Wheezing, gasping?
Anxious look?
Shock?
—YES→
Possible poisoning
or allergic reaction
See **Bites and stings** and
Poison – swallowed
See a vet NOW

NO↓

Coughing?
Blood-tinged sputum?
Smell of smoke?
—YES→
Smoke inhalation
See **Poison – inhaled**
See a vet NOW

NO↓

Panting intensely?
Glazed expression?
Exposed to heat?
—YES→
Heatstroke
See **Heatstroke**
See a vet NOW

NO↓

Abnormally light breathing?
Cherry-red gums?
Twitching muscles and fever?
—YES→
Carbon monoxide poisoning
See **Carbon monoxide**
See a vet NOW

NO↓
cont'd

83

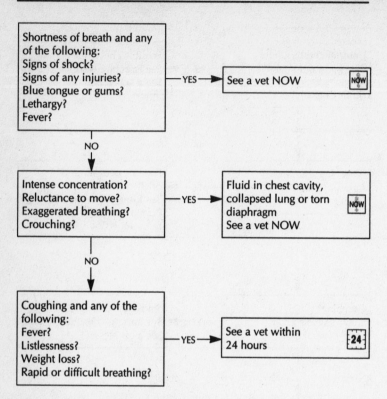

Shortness of breath and any of the following:
Signs of shock?
Signs of any injuries?
Blue tongue or gums?
Lethargy?
Fever?

— YES → See a vet NOW

— NO

Intense concentration?
Reluctance to move?
Exaggerated breathing?
Crouching?

— YES → Fluid in chest cavity, collapsed lung or torn diaphragm
See a vet NOW

— NO

Coughing and any of the following:
Fever?
Listlessness?
Weight loss?
Rapid or difficult breathing?

— YES → See a vet within 24 hours

ARTIFICIAL RESPIRATION

If your cat has stopped breathing:

1. Place the cat on its side. Clear the airway of debris and pull the tongue forward.

Fig. 1: Clear the airway

Any material blocking the throat or nose is removed.

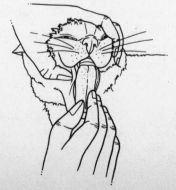

2. Close the cat's mouth. With your hand around the muzzle, place your mouth over the cat's nose and blow in until you see the chest expand.

Fig. 2: Breathe into the cat's lungs

Your hand on the muzzle
creates an airtight seal.

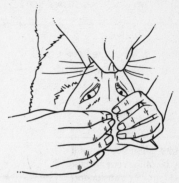

3. Take your mouth away and let the lungs deflate.
4. Repeat this procedure twenty to thirty times per minute.
5. Check the pulse every ten seconds to ensure the heart is still beating.
6. If the heart is not beating, give heart massage in conjunction with artificial respiration. (See page 13.)
7. Get professional veterinary attention as soon as possible.

BURNS AND SCALDS

Most burns are caused by hot liquids, fire and heat, but burns can also be caused by chemicals and electricity. The least severe burns result in superficial damage and can be treated at home. More severe burns inflict deeper damage, can lead to shock, sometimes even days later, and need immediate veterinary treatment. Do not underestimate the seriousness of burns. Burns to relatively small areas of the body can be life threatening.

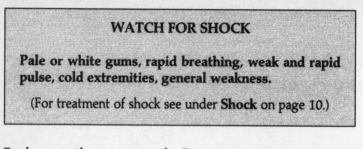

WATCH FOR SHOCK

Pale or white gums, rapid breathing, weak and rapid pulse, cold extremities, general weakness.

(For treatment of shock see under **Shock** on page 10.)

For burns to the eyes see under **Eye injuries** on page 106.
For burns inside the mouth see under **Mouth injuries** on page 125.

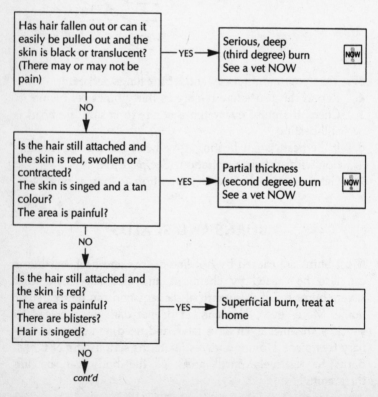

Has hair fallen out or can it easily be pulled out and the skin is black or translucent? (There may or may not be pain) —YES→ Serious, deep (third degree) burn See a vet NOW

NO

Is the hair still attached and the skin is red, swollen or contracted? The skin is singed and a tan colour? The area is painful? —YES→ Partial thickness (second degree) burn See a vet NOW

NO

Is the hair still attached and the skin is red? The area is painful? There are blisters? Hair is singed? —YES→ Superficial burn, treat at home

NO

cont'd

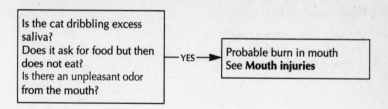

Is the cat dribbling excess saliva?
Does it ask for food but then does not eat?
Is there an unpleasant odor from the mouth?

—YES—▶ Probable burn in mouth
See **Mouth injuries**

- Do not apply ointments, creams, butter or margarine to burns. They do not help
- If a burn has been caused by chemicals, wear rubber gloves so that your hands are not burned

If the skin is intact and burned by heat (first degree burns):

1. Restrain the cat.
2. Flush the affected area with cool water as soon as possible by placing the cat in a bath or by using a gentle stream from a hose or shower attachment. (The faster you cool the area down, the less damage there will be.)

Fig. 1: Cool down the affected area

Flush the burn with lots of cool, clean water.

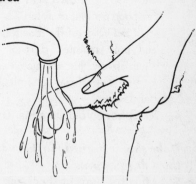

3. Apply a cold compress to the area (a bag of frozen vegetables) for twenty minutes.

Fig. 2: Apply a cool compress

The bag of frozen vegetables is compressed over the burn to reduce further tissue damage.

4. Cover with a non-stick bandage. The bandage protects the injured area and prevents the cat from licking it. Change the bandage daily. If it smells, get veterinary attention within twenty-four hours.

5. Telephone your veterinarian for further advice.

If the skin is intact and burned by chemicals:

1. Remove the cat's collar if it is contaminated.

2. Continue flushing the area for twenty minutes, making sure that the chemical washed off does not burn any other part of the cat's body. Use mild detergent or shampoo. In the case of known acid burns, rinse with baking soda (one teaspoon per pint of water).

    (If the inside of the mouth is burned, restrain the cat on its side and pour repeated cups of cool water through the mouth. Alternatively, flush the mouth using a garden hose.)

3. Cover superficial chemical burns with a non-sticking bandage.

4. Telephone your veterinarian for further advice.

If the skin is burned partly or totally through (second and third degree burns):

1. Look for signs of shock and treat if necessary.

2. Apply a clean, dry dressing to the burns. Avoid using cotton or other loose-fibred materials that stick to wounds.

3. Wrap torn sheeting or other soft material around the burned area.
4. Take the cat immediately to a veterinarian.

Reduce the risks of scalds and burns. Do not leave your cat unattended in the kitchen while you are cooking, it might step in a hot frying pan looking for food! Use a fire screen to prevent your cat getting too near an open fire.

CARBON MONOXIDE

Carbon monoxide poisoning may occur if propane gas heaters and cookers or indoor barbecues leak in unventilated places. Older cars without catalytic converters in their exhausts also emit carbon monoxide. Never put your cat in its carrier in the trunk of your car.

Do not put yourself in danger by trying to rescue a cat. Make sure you have fresh air to breathe.

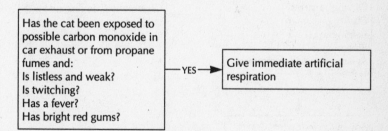

```
Has the cat been exposed to
possible carbon monoxide in
car exhaust or from propane
fumes and:                        ──YES──▶   Give immediate artificial
Is listless and weak?                        respiration
Is twitching?
Has a fever?
Has bright red gums?
```

If the cat has stopped breathing:
1. Remove it from further danger.
2. Give artificial respiration if breathing has stopped.
3. Give CPR if breathing and the heart have both stopped.
4. If breathing resumes, contact your veterinarian for further advice.

5. When possible, continue CPR on the way to getting immediate veterinary attention.

CHOKING

Cats are usually careful about what they put in their mouths but bones sometimes get stuck on teeth or flat against the hard palate, causing the cat to paw at its mouth. If a bone or any other object blocks the windpipe, choking follows. If your cat is choking, do not wait for veterinary help. Your cat risks suffocating to death.

For foreign bodies stuck in the mouth not causing choking see **Mouth injuries** on page 125.

Choking is frightening. An otherwise calm cat is liable to scratch and bite. Take extra care to avoid getting injured.

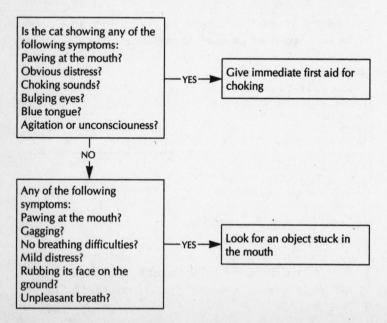

Is the cat showing any of the following symptoms:
Pawing at the mouth?
Obvious distress?
Choking sounds?
Bulging eyes?
Blue tongue?
Agitation or unconsciouness?

—YES→ Give immediate first aid for choking

NO ↓

Any of the following symptoms:
Pawing at the mouth?
Gagging?
No breathing difficulties?
Mild distress?
Rubbing its face on the ground?
Unpleasant breath?

—YES→ Look for an object stuck in the mouth

If the cat is conscious:

1. Restrain the cat by wrapping it in a towel with only its head visible.
2. Open the mouth by grasping the upper jaw with one hand and pressing the lips over the upper teeth.

Fig. 1: Open the mouth

The thumb presses on one side and the fingers on the other so the upper lips cover the teeth.

3. Open the mouth with your other hand.
4. Use a blunt instrument or the handle of a spoon to pry the object off the teeth or from the roof of the mouth. (Do not pull on a visible thread or string. It may be attached to an object in the stomach.)

Fig. 2: Pry out the object

A blunt instrument is slipped behind the object to loosen it and bring it forward.

If the cat is unconscious or is still choking and you cannot see the object:

1. Hold the cat by its thighs and gently shake and swing it.

Fig. 3: Shake the cat

The thighs are held firmly.
Swinging allows gravity to assist.
If this is not successful after one
minute, apply abdominal
pressure.

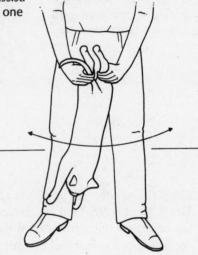

2. Place the cat on its side.
3. Using one hand to support the back, grab the abdomen just behind the ribs and squeeze upwards and forwards towards the throat. (This is a variation of the Heimlich maneuver you would use on a person choking. Too much pressure can cause internal bleeding.)
4. Sweep your fingers through the mouth and remove the dislodged object. Take care you are not bitten.
5. Give artificial respiration or CPR as necessary.
6. If artificial respiration or CPR is necessary, get immediate veterinary assistance.

COMA

When a cat appears to be asleep but has no pain response it is in a coma. Comas are most common in diabetic cats but can also be caused by extremes of temperature, certain drugs and poisons, overwhelming infections and shock.

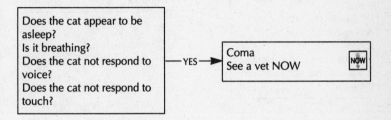

Does the cat appear to be asleep?
Is it breathing?
Does the cat not respond to voice?
Does the cat not respond to touch?

— YES →

Coma
See a vet NOW NOW

1. Make sure the airway is not blocked.
2. Eliminate or treat the specific cause of the coma if this is known.
3. Monitor breathing and heart.
4. Provide artificial respiration or CPR if necessary.
5. Seek veterinary help immediately.

CONSTIPATION

The most common cause of constipation is a hairball, a tangled matt of hair and feces that are too dry to pass easily through the anus. Constipation is also caused by slower intestinal movements, hernias, tumors, and bone or grass that has been swallowed. Disease affecting the nerves that control the intestines can also lead to severe constipation. Severe diarrhea causes straining that can be mistaken for constipation.

93

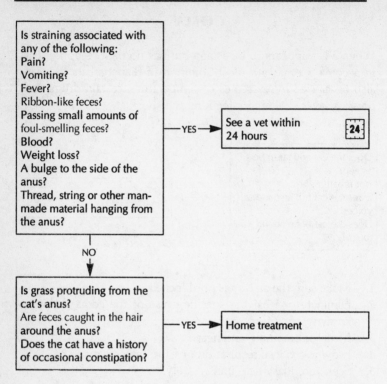

Is straining associated with any of the following:
Pain?
Vomiting?
Fever?
Ribbon-like feces?
Passing small amounts of foul-smelling feces?
Blood?
Weight loss?
A bulge to the side of the anus?
Thread, string or other man-made material hanging from the anus?

—YES→ See a vet within 24 hours

NO

Is grass protruding from the cat's anus?
Are feces caught in the hair around the anus?
Does the cat have a history of occasional constipation?

—YES→ Home treatment

1. If grass is visible at the anal opening, put on a rubber glove and gently ease it out. **Do not attempt to pull out string or thread**, you may cause serious internal damage.

2. If feces are stuck in the hair around the anus, trim the hair and matted feces away with scissors. Wash the inflamed anal region with warm soapy water and apply soothing water-soluble (K-Y) jelly.

3. If there is a history of intermittent constipation, add mineral oil to the cat's food at a dose rate of 1 teaspoon per 5 Kg (11 lbs) body weight. (Do not give mineral oil directly by mouth. If it gets in the lungs, which it can easily do, it may cause pneumonia.)

4. Take your cat's temperature. If it is elevated, if there is blood on the thermometer or the thermometer hits a hard

blockage, take your cat to your veterinarian within twenty-four hours. Your cat may be hospitalized and given enemas to relieve the constipation.

Constipation is more common in older than younger cats. Use purpose made laxatives when necessary to keep stools softer. Make sure your cat has adequate water to drink. Never try to give an enema without contacting your veterinarian and following explicit instructions.

CONVULSIONS AND SEIZURES

Convulsions or seizures cause a cat to appear to lose control of its body. If seizures recur, the condition is usually called epilepsy. Although there are many known causes of convulsions, such as low blood sugar, liver disease, low blood calcium, poor circulation, viral and bacterial infections, poisons, scar tissue on the brain and brain tumors, in many instances it is very difficult to determine the exact cause.

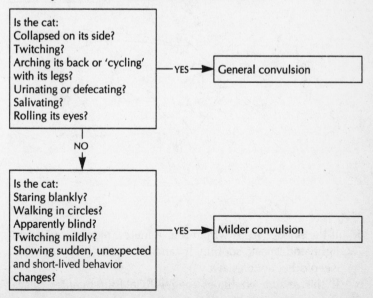

Is the cat:
Collapsed on its side?
Twitching?
Arching its back or 'cycling' with its legs?
Urinating or defecating?
Salivating?
Rolling its eyes?

— YES → General convulsion

NO ↓

Is the cat:
Staring blankly?
Walking in circles?
Apparently blind?
Twitching mildly?
Showing sudden, unexpected and short-lived behavior changes?

— YES → Milder convulsion

CONVULSIONS AND SEIZURES

If a cat has a seizure, do not panic. Most convulsions are not life threatening. Avoid the cat only if you are in an area where rabies exists and you do not know the vaccination status of the cat.

1. Cats rarely choke on their tongues. Avoid putting your fingers near the cat's mouth unless absolutely necessary.
2. If your cat is having a mild convulsion, gain its attention. This might prevent a full seizure from developing.
3. If a full seizure has developed, get a blanket or cushions.
4. Pull the cat away from articles it may injure itself on and wrap the cat in the blanket or surround it with cushions to protect it from self-inflicted injuries.

Fig. 1: Protect the cat

Cushions surround the cat to prevent rolling and protect it from hard surfaces.

5. If the seizure stops within four minutes, reduce sound and light and speak soothingly and reassuringly to the cat. Keep other animals away.
6. If the seizure continues longer than four minutes, place

the cat in a covered container and take it to the veterinarian immediately.

7. Keep a record of the time the seizure occurred and what the cat was doing before it happened. This helps the diagnosis if further seizures occur.

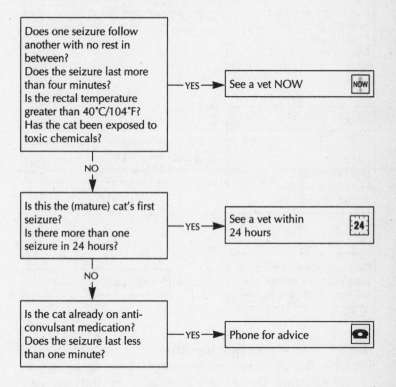

Does one seizure follow another with no rest in between?
Does the seizure last more than four minutes?
Is the rectal temperature greater than 40°C/104°F?
Has the cat been exposed to toxic chemicals?

— YES ➤ See a vet NOW [NOW]

NO

Is this the (mature) cat's first seizure?
Is there more than one seizure in 24 hours?

— YES ➤ See a vet within 24 hours [24]

NO

Is the cat already on anti-convulsant medication?
Does the seizure last less than one minute?

— YES ➤ Phone for advice [☎]

COUGHING

Coughing is a defence mechanism to remove unwanted material from the air passages. Coughing can be caused by allergy and pollution, but also by infections, worms, heart problems, chest disease, tumors, or by fluid pressing on the lungs. Some causes of coughing can be treated at home. Others require veterinary attention.

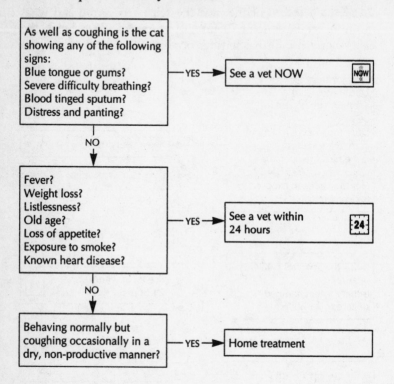

As well as coughing is the cat showing any of the following signs:
Blue tongue or gums?
Severe difficulty breathing?
Blood tinged sputum?
Distress and panting?

— YES → See a vet NOW

NO

Fever?
Weight loss?
Listlessness?
Old age?
Loss of appetite?
Exposure to smoke?
Known heart disease?

— YES → See a vet within 24 hours

NO

Behaving normally but coughing occasionally in a dry, non-productive manner?

— YES → Home treatment

Home treatment for minor coughs:

1. Give the cat a proprietary cough syrup containing an expectorant. (Do not give a cough syrup that suppresses coughing.)
2. Turn on the hot shower in the bathroom and fill the room with steam. If it is not distressed by your doing so, leave the cat in the steam filled room for up to fifteen minutes.
3. If the cough is not improving by the third day or if the cat appears unwell in any other way, get veterinary advice.

DIABETIC EMERGENCIES

Emergencies can occur when either too much or too little insulin is injected into a diabetic cat. Both are major emergencies. If untreated they can lead to coma and rapid death.

TOO MUCH INSULIN

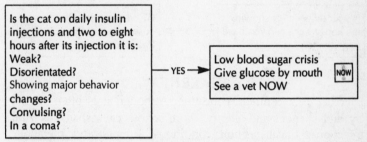

Is the cat on daily insulin injections and two to eight hours after its injection it is:
Weak?
Disorientated?
Showing major behavior changes?
Convulsing?
In a coma?

— YES →

Low blood sugar crisis
Give glucose by mouth NOW
See a vet NOW

If a cat is diabetic, always keep glucose, corn syrup or honey available for emergency use when too much insulin is injected.

1. At the first sign of an insulin overdose and depressed blood sugar, syringe liquid glucose into the cat's mouth.
2. If the cat is convulsing, lift the lips and rub glucose syrup on the gums.
3. Because this may be only the beginning of the low sugar crisis, get immediate veterinary help. (Your veterinarian may give glucose intravenously.)

NOT ENOUGH INSULIN

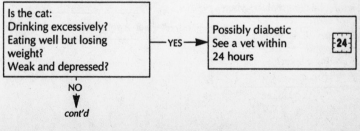

Is the cat:
Drinking excessively?
Eating well but losing weight?
Weak and depressed?

— YES →

Possibly diabetic
See a vet within 24 hours [24]

NO
↓
cont'd

DIARRHEA

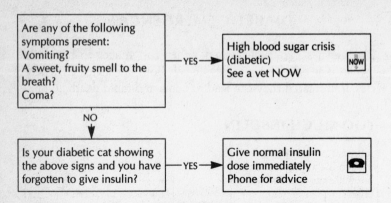

Are any of the following symptoms present:
Vomiting?
A sweet, fruity smell to the breath?
Coma?

—YES→ High blood sugar crisis (diabetic)
See a vet NOW **NOW**

NO

Is your diabetic cat showing the above signs and you have forgotten to give insulin?

—YES→ Give normal insulin dose immediately
Phone for advice

DIARRHEA

Diarrhea is a common condition. Although it is often caused by diet changes and allergy, more serious causes such as viral infections, malabsorption conditions, tumors and metabolic failures all cause severe or persistent loose stools.

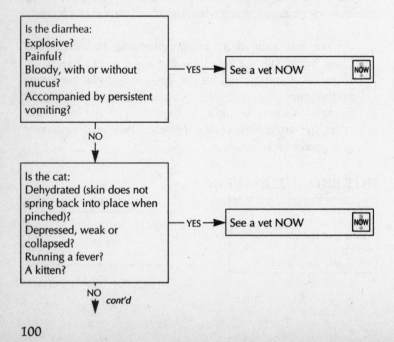

Is the diarrhea:
Explosive?
Painful?
Bloody, with or without mucus?
Accompanied by persistent vomiting?

—YES→ See a vet NOW **NOW**

NO

Is the cat:
Dehydrated (skin does not spring back into place when pinched)?
Depressed, weak or collapsed?
Running a fever?
A kitten?

—YES→ See a vet NOW **NOW**

NO *cont'd*

100

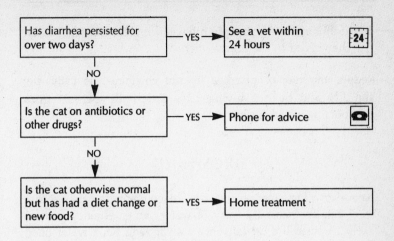

Diarrhea with no vomiting:
1. Remove all food. Allow the drinking of plenty of water to prevent dehydration.
2. Give kaolin mixture, one teaspoon per 5 Kg (11 lbs) body weight every six hours.
3. If diarrhea persists for more than twenty-four hours or if blood appears, telephone your veterinarian.
4. After a twelve-hour fast, give the cat a small quantity of cooked chicken. Continue with this diet until stools return to normal.

Diarrhea with mild vomiting:
1. Remove all food and water for twelve hours.
2. Give the cat ice cubes to lick or a teaspoon of soda water every hour.
3. When vomiting has stopped for twelve hours, feed the cat a small quantity of cooked chicken and reintroduce small quantities of water. If there is no further vomiting, feed a little more food two hours later and give kaolin mixture to coat the stomach.

4. Continue this treatment until well formed stools are passed then revert to the normal diet.

Reduce the risk of diarrhea by not changing the cat's diet abruptly and by not giving table scraps. If your cat goes outdoors, worm it routinely.

DROWNING

Near-drowning emergencies are not common in cats because most cats are naturally wary of water. An emergency is most likely to occur if a cat falls into a swimming pool, water filled tank or canal from which it cannot get out.

1. Rescue the cat.
2. If the cat is conscious, wrap it in a towel and keep it warm.
3. If the cat is unconscious, drain the lungs of water by holding it upside down for ten to twenty seconds, giving several downward shakes.

Fig. 1: Draining a cat's lungs

Hold the cat just above its knees and shake out water from the air passages and lungs, by swinging it from side to side and lifting up and down.

4. Position the cat on its side with its head lower than its lungs. Clear debris from the mouth and pull out the tongue.

5. Check for a heartbeat. If there is none, begin CPR.
6. If the heart is beating but the cat is not breathing, give artificial respiration.

Serious life threatening problems can occur hours after a near-drowning incident. Take the cat for immediate veterinary attention.

WATCH FOR SHOCK

Pale or white gums, rapid breathing, weak and rapid pulse, cold extremities, general weakness.

(For treatment of shock see under **Shock** on page 10.)

EAR INJURIES

Sudden, violent head shaking is usually caused by a foreign object in the ear. Head shaking itself can rupture a blood vessel in the ear causing the flap to swell like a balloon and fill with blood.

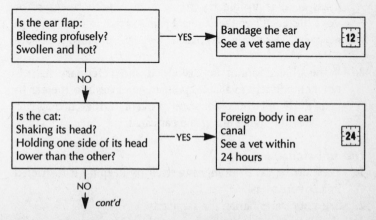

Is the ear flap:
Bleeding profusely?
Swollen and hot?

— YES → Bandage the ear
See a vet same day **12**

NO ↓

Is the cat:
Shaking its head?
Holding one side of its head lower than the other?

— YES → Foreign body in ear canal
See a vet within 24 hours **24**

NO ↓ *cont'd*

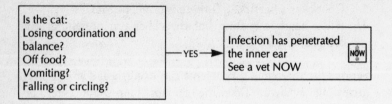

Is the cat:
Losing coordination and
balance?
Off food?
Vomiting?
Falling or circling?

— YES → Infection has penetrated
the inner ear
See a vet NOW | NOW |

Bleeding ear:
1. Apply pressure with absorbent pads on both sides of the ear flap for several minutes.
2. See your veterinarian the same day.

Swollen ear:
The most likely cause of a swollen ear is an abscess.

1. Correct the underlying cause of head shaking by seeing your veterinarian in the next twenty-four hours to treat the abscess or to eliminate mites, foreign bodies, infection or allergy.

Head shaking:
1. Look in the ear closest to the ground. If an object like a grass seed is visible try to remove it with tweezers or your fingers. (If you see a round purple object do not attempt to remove it. This is a benign tumour. Surgery is required to remove it.)
2. If the object cannot be dislodged and veterinary help is not immediately available, pour mineral oil into the ear to help flush out the object and prevent further damage to the sensitive tissue lining the ear canal.

Loss of balance:
1. Frevent the cat from injuring itself by keeping it restricted in a covered basket.
2. See your veterinarian the same day.

ELECTRIC SHOCK

Electric shock can cause cardiac arrest. It also burns the affected part of the body. Although chewing on electric cords is the most common cause of electrocution, contacts with power lines and lightning strikes also cause usually fatal accidents.

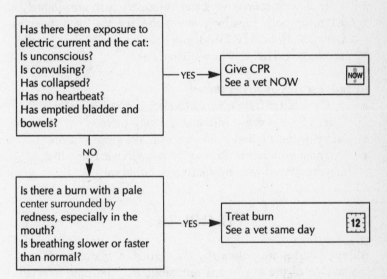

Has there been exposure to electric current and the cat:
Is unconscious?
Is convulsing?
Has collapsed?
Has no heartbeat?
Has emptied bladder and bowels?

— YES → Give CPR
See a vet NOW | NOW

NO ↓

Is there a burn with a pale center surrounded by redness, especially in the mouth?
Is breathing slower or faster than normal?

— YES → Treat burn
See a vet same day | 12

WATCH FOR SHOCK

Pale or white gums, rapid breathing, weak and rapid pulse, cold extremities, general weakness.

(For treatment of shock see under **Shock** on page 10.)

---

1. Do not put your life at risk. If the cat is rigid it may be fatal to touch it. Avoid touching fluids in contact with the cat. Turn off electricity at source. If this is not possible,

use a non-metal broom handle to move the cat well away from the exposed electric current.

2. Check whether the cat's heart is beating and it is breathing.
3. Give artificial respiration or CPR as necessary.
4. If there are only mouth burns, treat with cold compresses to reduce further damage.
5. Even if your cat recovers, get veterinary help immediately. Monitor both breathing and pulse for the next twelve hours. (Potentially fatal shock may occur hours after an apparently uncomplicated recovery from electrocution.)

Reduce the risk of electrocution:

- Apply a bitter tasting spray to electric cords to deter kittens from playing with and chewing them
- Never leave a kitten in a room with live electric cords
- Examine your home. Reposition any electric cords that may be played with by a kitten or bored cat

EYE INJURIES

All eye injuries are potentially dangerous. A minor scratch to the surface of the eye, if left untreated, may become infected and lead to loss of vision. Do not take chances with a cat's sight. Whenever an eye is injured arrange for a veterinary examination.

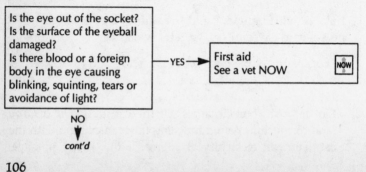

Is the eye out of the socket?
Is the surface of the eyeball damaged?
Is there blood or a foreign body in the eye causing blinking, squinting, tears or avoidance of light?

— YES → First aid
See a vet NOW   NOW

NO

↓

cont'd

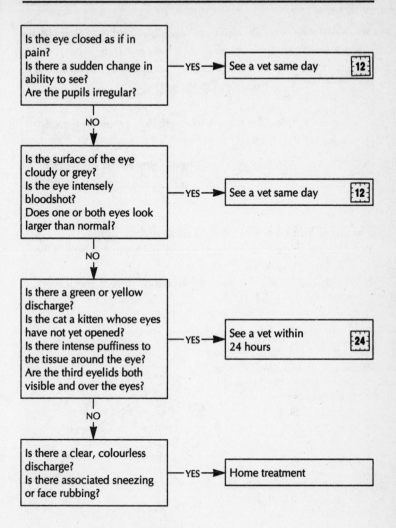

Is the eye closed as if in pain?
Is there a sudden change in ability to see?
Are the pupils irregular? ——YES——▶ See a vet same day 〔12〕

NO ▼

Is the surface of the eye cloudy or grey?
Is the eye intensely bloodshot?
Does one or both eyes look larger than normal? ——YES——▶ See a vet same day 〔12〕

NO ▼

Is there a green or yellow discharge?
Is the cat a kitten whose eyes have not yet opened?
Is there intense puffiness to the tissue around the eye?
Are the third eyelids both visible and over the eyes? ——YES——▶ See a vet within 24 hours 〔24〕

NO ▼

Is there a clear, colourless discharge?
Is there associated sneezing or face rubbing? ——YES——▶ Home treatment

The eye is out of the socket:

1. Do not attempt to push the eye back in.
2. Cover with a clean, damp cloth or sponge soaked in salty warm water or in a supersaturated sugar solution. Loosely bandage this to the head.

3. Keep the cat as quiet as possible and get immediate veterinary help. (Minutes count if the eye is to be saved.)

WATCH FOR SHOCK

Pale or white gums, rapid breathing, weak and rapid pulse, cold extremities, general weakness.

(For treatment of shock see under **Shock** on page 10.)

The cat is blinking, squinting and avoiding light:
1. Lift the upper lid by retracting it with your thumb. Check for foreign objects.
2. With the thumb of your other hand, retract the lower lid and check for debris.

Fig. 1: Retract the lids

While the thumbs pull back and lift the upper and lower eyelids, the other fingers control head movements.

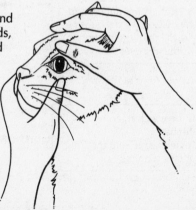

3. If there is a non-penetrating foreign object, remove it by flushing the eye with tepid water.
4. Alternatively, use a cotton swab moistened with water to ease the irritant out of the eye.

Fig. 2: Flush with water

The eye is flushed with copious
fresh water to dislodge the
object.

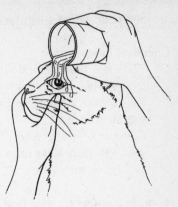

5. If you cannot remove the irritant, cover the eye in a
    bandage to prevent further injury and get immediate
    veterinary help.
6. If there is a penetrating foreign object, do not attempt to
    remove it. Bandage the eye or put a protective Elizabethan
    collar on your cat and get immediate veterinary
    assistance.

The eye is red, there is squinting and tear production but no foreign body:

1. If the eye has been scratched, cover it with a clean damp
    cloth.
2. Prevent self-inflicted damage by applying an Elizabethan
    collar or bandaging the dew claws.

Fig. 3: Bandaged dew claws

Light bandages reduce the risk
of damage from sharp dew claws
if the cat paws at its eyes.

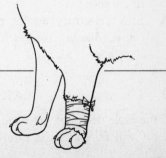

3.   See your veterinarian the same day.

Chemical burns:
1.   Wash out the chemical with lots of fresh water for at least ten minutes.
2.   Follow instructions on the chemical packaging for more specific treatment.
3.   Cover the eye to prevent self-inflicted damage and see your veterinarian as soon as possible, taking the chemical's packaging with you.

Torn, bruised or swollen eyelids from a fight or by trauma:
1.   Apply a cold compress for ten minutes to reduce swelling.
2.   See your veterinarian within twenty-four hours.
3.   Use an Elizabethan collar or dew claw bandages to prevent further self-inflicted damage.

Green or yellow discharge:
1.   Infection is present. Clean the eyes with tepid water, a proprietary eyewash or dilute cold tea.
2.   Watch for other signs of illness such as sneezing and loss of appetite. See your veterinarian within twenty-four hours.

Watery discharge:
1.   Check for foreign bodies.
2.   Flush the eyes with tepid water, proprietary eye wash or dilute cold tea.
3.   Seek veterinary advice on how to treat the underlying cause. (Allergies, blocked tear ducts and eyelid defects all cause chronic tear production.)

FAINTING

If the brain does not get enough oxygen or sugar temporarily, a cat will faint. This is rare but most likely to occur in flat faced breeds like Persians. Coughing fits, heart disease and low blood sugar can all cause fainting.

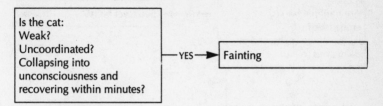

Is the cat:
Weak?
Uncoordinated?
Collapsing into
unconsciousness and
recovering within minutes?

— YES ➔ Fainting

If a cat has fainted:
1. Pull the tongue forward to maintain a clear air passage.

Fig. 1: Pull the cat's tongue forward

2. Check the gums to make sure there are no signs of shock or heart failure.
3. Keep the cat quiet for an hour after fainting.
4. Keep a record of when, where and for how long fainting occurs. If there is a repeat episode, telephone your veterinarian for advice.

FISH-HOOKS

Fishing lures smell delightful and often have delicacies like minnows or frogs attached to them. Unfortunately, cats can get the hooks embedded in their lips and paws.

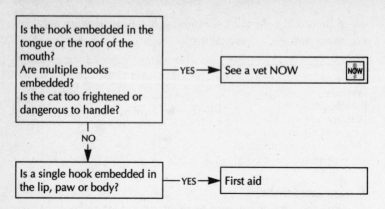

| Is the hook embedded in the tongue or the roof of the mouth? Are multiple hooks embedded? Is the cat too frightened or dangerous to handle? | →YES→ | See a vet NOW |

NO ↓

| Is a single hook embedded in the lip, paw or body? | →YES→ | First aid |

1. Restrain the cat in a blanket and, if you can, wrap gauze around the face as a temporary muzzle, avoiding the lip area in which the hook is embedded.
2. If the barbed end of the hook is visible, cut it off with wire cutters then pull the remaining part of the hook back out in the same direction it entered.

Fig. 1: Cut the barb

If there is tension when you try to retract the hook after you have cut off the barb, stop pulling and get immediate veterinary help.

3. If the barb is not visible, use pliers to push the hook through the skin, exposing the barb.
4. Cut off the barb and retract the hook.
5. Clean the wound thoroughly with 3% hydrogen peroxide.
6. Telephone your veterinarian for further advice.

- Never pull on fishing line hanging from a cat's mouth. This may cause severe damage
- Never cut the fishing line 'leader'. Leave as much line attached as is practical
- Take the cat to your veterinarian for an immediate X-ray for swallowed hooks

FROSTBITE AND HYPOTHERMIA

Exposure to extreme cold can chill the whole body. This is hypothermia. If core temperature drops catastrophically, life is threatened. Most cats are protected from severe cold by their dense fur. The extremities, like the tips of the ears and tail, have least protection and can suffer from local freezing, or frostbite.

WATCH FOR SHOCK

Pale or white gums, rapid breathing, weak and rapid pulse, cold extremities, general weakness.

(For treatment of shock see under **Shock** on page 10.)

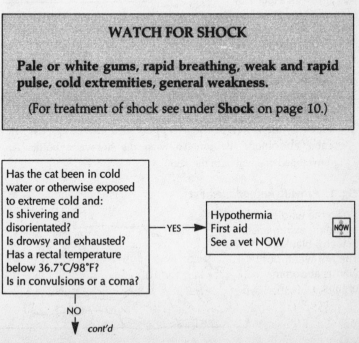

Has the cat been in cold water or otherwise exposed to extreme cold and:
Is shivering and disorientated?
Is drowsy and exhausted?
Has a rectal temperature below 36.7°C/98°F?
Is in convulsions or a coma?

→ YES → Hypothermia
First aid
See a vet NOW   NOW

NO
↓ cont'd

FROSTBITE AND HYPOTHERMIA

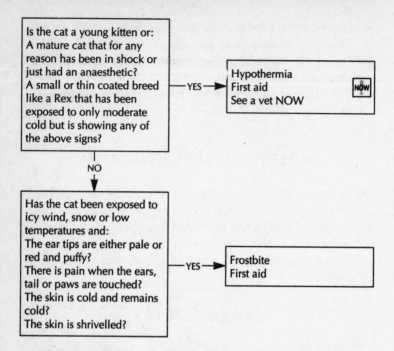

Is the cat a young kitten or:
A mature cat that for any reason has been in shock or just had an anaesthetic?
A small or thin coated breed like a Rex that has been exposed to only moderate cold but is showing any of the above signs?

—YES→

Hypothermia
First aid
See a vet NOW

NOW

NO

Has the cat been exposed to icy wind, snow or low temperatures and:
The ear tips are either pale or red and puffy?
There is pain when the ears, tail or paws are touched?
The skin is cold and remains cold?
The skin is shrivelled?

—YES→

Frostbite
First aid

For hypothermia:

1. Wrap the cat in warm blankets. (Warm the blankets quickly in your clothes drier.)

2. Place a hot-water bottle wrapped in a towel against the cat's abdomen. (Be sure to wrap the hot-water bottle. An unwrapped one will burn the skin.)

Fig. 1: Provide immediate heat

Wrap the whole body, including extremities, in warm blankets. The hot-water bottle warms abdominal organs.

3. If the cat is conscious, give warmed fluids to drink.
4. Take the cat's temperature every ten minutes. If it is below 36.7°C/98°F, get immediate veterinary help. Once it is above 37.8°C/100°F, remove the hot-water bottle but keep the cat in a warm room. (Avoid overheating the cat.)

For frostbite:
1. After exposure to extreme cold examine the feet, ears and tail for paleness and signs of frostbite.
2. Massage the areas gently with a warm towel. (Do not rub hard or squeeze. This can further damage the affected tissue.)
3. Warm the frozen parts with tepid water heated to a maximum of 32.2°C/90°F. As thawing occurs, the skin becomes reddened.
4. If the skin turns dark, get immediate veterinary help.

HEART FAILURE

Sudden heart failure is uncommon in cats, although more common than was once thought. In most instances sudden heart failure is secondary to some other major crisis. That crisis must be overcome if the cat is to survive.

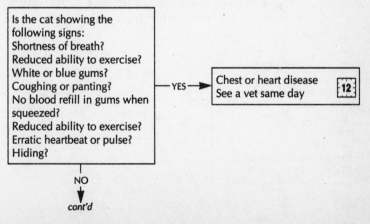

Is the cat showing the following signs:
Shortness of breath?
Reduced ability to exercise?
White or blue gums?
Coughing or panting?
No blood refill in gums when squeezed?
Reduced ability to exercise?
Erratic heartbeat or pulse?
Hiding?

— YES → Chest or heart disease
See a vet same day   **12**

NO
↓
cont'd

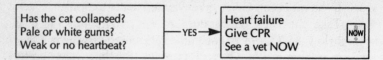

| Has the cat collapsed?
Pale or white gums?
Weak or no heartbeat? | —YES→ | Heart failure
Give CPR
See a vet NOW | NOW |

For heart failure:

1. Feel for a heartbeat or pulse. Squeeze the gums and see if the squeezed area refills with blood when you remove your finger.

2. If it does, the heart is still pumping. Give artificial respiration if necessary and get immediate veterinary help.

3. If the heart is not pumping, start heart massage and artificial respiration (CPR). Get immediate veterinary help.

See **Artificial respiration** and **Heart massage** on pages 14–15.

HEATSTROKE

Cats eliminate excess body heat by sweating through their pads and panting. If the surrounding temperature is too high, these methods of losing heat become ineffective. Body temperature rises rapidly. Death follows quickly if body temperature is not immediately reduced. Cats are attracted to the warm interior of clothes dryers. Always check your dryer before closing the door and turning it on. Fatal heatstroke can occur if your cat is locked inside.

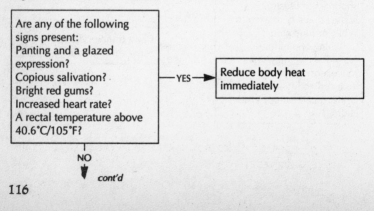

| Are any of the following signs present:
Panting and a glazed expression?
Copious salivation?
Bright red gums?
Increased heart rate?
A rectal temperature above 40.6°C/105°F? | —YES→ | Reduce body heat immediately |

NO ↓ *cont'd*

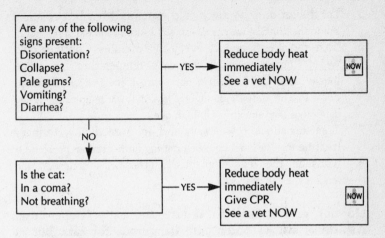

Are any of the following signs present: Disorientation? Collapse? Pale gums? Vomiting? Diarrhea?	—YES→	Reduce body heat immediately See a vet NOW

NO ↓

Is the cat: In a coma? Not breathing?	—YES→	Reduce body heat immediately Give CPR See a vet NOW

1. Remove the cat from the hot environment.
2. Put the cat in the sink or bath. Run a shower over the cat, especially on its head, allowing water to fill the sink or bath.

Fig. 1: Immerse in cold water

The cat's head is held above the water.

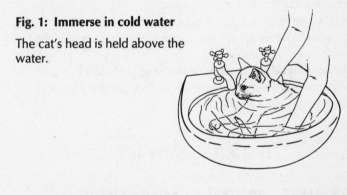

3. Alternatively, hose down the cat with a garden hose or place it in a pool of water. (Do not put the cat's head under water. If it is unconscious, make sure no water enters the nose or mouth.)
4. Apply a packet of frozen vegetables to the head to reduce heat to the brain.

117

5. Let the cat drink as much cold water as it wants. (A pinch of salt in the drinking water replaces salt lost through panting.)

6. Take rectal temperature every five minutes. Continue cold water immersion until the cat's temperature has fallen below 39.4°C/103°F. (Do not worry if the temperature drops down to 37.8°C/100°F or slightly less. A lower temperature is less dangerous than an extremely high one.)

7. Treat for shock if necessary and get immediate veterinary treatment. (The brain can swell causing further serious problems.)

8. Massage the legs vigorously. (This helps circulation and reduces the risk of shock.)

Do not give aspirin to reduce the cat's temperature. Aspirin is always potentially dangerous for cats, but in these circumstances even more so.

Prevent heatstroke:
- Always provide your cat with good ventilation, access to shade and plenty of water to drink
- Never leave your cat in a car on a warm day
- In winter, never leave your cat in a car in direct sunlight with the heater on
- In warm weather, make sure flat nosed cats like Persians, old and fat cats have access to cool rooms and plenty of water

INJURIES – SURFACE

ABRASIONS – BRUISES – LACERATIONS

Injuries to the skin are common. Unpleasant abrasions occur if the skin is scraped on a hard surface. Bruises develop after more traumatic accidents when blood vessels under the skin are damaged. Skin cuts or lacerations occur most frequently to the feet, especially the pads, but can occur anywhere. If your cat shows signs of these superficial injuries, carry out a complete examination for potentially more serious, deeper damage.

WATCH FOR SHOCK

Pale or white gums, rapid breathing, weak and rapid pulse, cold extremities, general weakness.

(For treatment of shock see under **Shock** on page 10.)

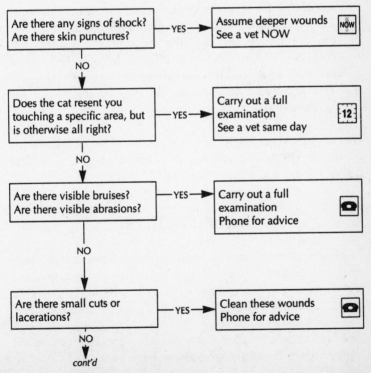

Are there any signs of shock? Are there skin punctures?	—YES→	Assume deeper wounds See a vet NOW
↓ NO		
Does the cat resent you touching a specific area, but is otherwise all right?	—YES→	Carry out a full examination See a vet same day
↓ NO		
Are there visible bruises? Are there visible abrasions?	—YES→	Carry out a full examination Phone for advice
↓ NO		
Are there small cuts or lacerations?	—YES→	Clean these wounds Phone for advice

NO
cont'd

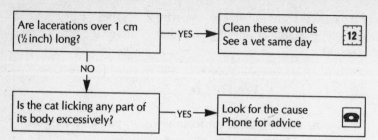

1.   Flush superficial wounds that are dirty with earth, rust, dust, plant material or animal saliva with 3% hydrogen peroxide or a non-stinging antiseptic diluted in warm water. (Do not use absorbent cotton wool. Fibres of this material might stick to the wound.)

2.   Apply a cold compress (bag of frozen vegetables or cold wet towel) for several minutes to bruised areas. (If a joint or paw is bruised and swollen, assume there are deeper injuries.)

3.   Do not try to bandage the wound. It is usually not necessary and is extremely difficult to do. Use a non-dusty cat litter until the wound heals.

4.   Telephone your veterinarian, describe the injury and get further advice.

Do not let the cat lick its wounds excessively. Cat saliva does contain an ingredient that acts as a mild antiseptic, so a little licking is cleansing and does no harm.

INJURIES – DEEP

Treat any deep wound as potentially life threatening. Deep wounds accompany penetrating injuries from knives, gunshot and impalement. They may also occur without any visible surface injuries after traffic accidents, falls and other trauma.

First aid for deep injuries that accompany penetrating wounds is given under **Puncture wounds** on page 146.

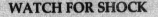

WATCH FOR SHOCK

Pale or white gums, rapid breathing, weak and rapid pulse, cold extremities, general weakness.

(For treatment of shock see under **Shock** on page 10.)

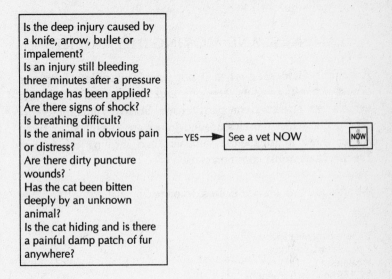

Is the deep injury caused by a knife, arrow, bullet or impalement?
Is an injury still bleeding three minutes after a pressure bandage has been applied?
Are there signs of shock?
Is breathing difficult?
Is the animal in obvious pain or distress?
Are there dirty puncture wounds?
Has the cat been bitten deeply by an unknown animal?
Is the cat hiding and is there a painful damp patch of fur anywhere?

— YES ⟶ See a vet NOW   NOW

1. Do not remove any penetrating objects such as arrows. (Removal may cause fatal internal bleeding. Always try to move the cat **with** the article it has impaled itself on. If this is not possible, try to get on-site immediate veterinary help. If this cannot be done, be prepared for possible fatal consequences when the cat is removed from the impaling object.

2. Calm the cat, apply pressure to control bleeding. Keep the airway open. Give CPR if necessary.

3. Assume that shock will occur. Wrap the cat in a blanket to keep it warm and get immediate veterinary help.

Remember, deep injuries such as concussion, torn diaphragms, ruptured bladders and hemorrhages from torn organs or blood vessels can occur without any visible superficial damage. If you know your cat has had a traumatic accident or if you see signs of shock while giving a head-to-tail examination after you have found signs of superficial injuries, get immediate veterinary help. See **Puncture wounds** on page 146 for further information.

LAMENESS AND MOVING DIFFICULTIES

A bone is **dislocated** when it pops out of its joint. A **sprain** occurs when ligaments, tendons and their associated blood vessels are stretched or partly torn. **Strains**, uncommon in cats, occur when muscles around joints are stretched or torn. All of these injuries cause lameness and moving difficulties. Trauma is the most common cause.

If bones are broken, see **Bones** on page 78.

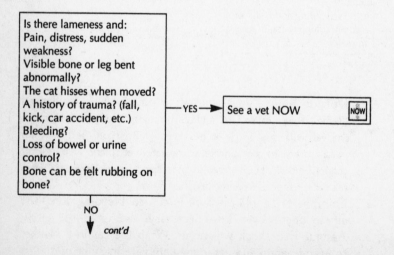

Is there lameness and:
Pain, distress, sudden weakness?
Visible bone or leg bent abnormally?
The cat hisses when moved?
A history of trauma? (fall, kick, car accident, etc.)
Bleeding?
Loss of bowel or urine control?
Bone can be felt rubbing on bone?

— YES ➔ See a vet NOW | NOW

NO
↓
cont'd

LAMENESS

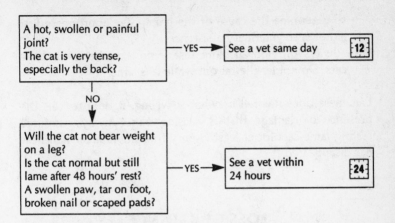

A hot, swollen or painful joint? The cat is very tense, especially the back? — YES → See a vet same day **12**

NO ↓

Will the cat not bear weight on a leg? Is the cat normal but still lame after 48 hours' rest? A swollen paw, tar on foot, broken nail or scaped pads? — YES → See a vet within 24 hours **24**

WATCH FOR SHOCK

Pale or white gums, rapid breathing, weak and rapid pulse, cold extremities, general weakness.

(For treatment of shock see under **Shock** on page 10.)

1. Restrain the cat if necessary and move it as little as possible.
2. If there are no obvious fractures and the cat can walk, do not attempt to splint the leg.
3. If there is severe pain or swelling, place the cat in a transport box and get immediate veterinary help.
4. Cradle the back of cats with back pain. Keep the cat's back straight by supporting its weight in front of the shoulders and behind the hips.
5. If immediate veterinary attention is not necessary, apply a cold compress (bag of frozen vegetables) to the swollen joint. (If the swelling is over twenty-four hours old, apply a warm compress.)
6. Carry out an examination of the affected part of the body

123

to determine the cause of the limp. Give appropriate first aid or seek veterinary assistance.

7. Always provide absolute rest — no exercise — for lame cats. Do not let the cat out while it is lame.

Lameness does not tell us what is wrong, it only reveals the presence of damage that is causing pain. Always continue resting lame cats for at least twenty-four hours **after** lameness has disappeared.

LOSS OF BALANCE

Sudden loss of balance may be caused by the early stages of brain concussion, by diabetic crisis, by shock or by spreading ear or throat infection or by a spontaneous disorder of the area of the brain responsible for balance (vestibular disease).

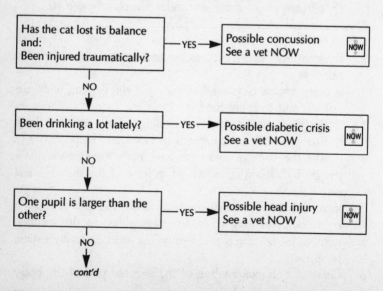

Has the cat lost its balance and:
Been injured traumatically? —YES→ Possible concussion See a vet NOW

NO

Been drinking a lot lately? —YES→ Possible diabetic crisis See a vet NOW

NO

One pupil is larger than the other? —YES→ Possible head injury See a vet NOW

NO

cont'd

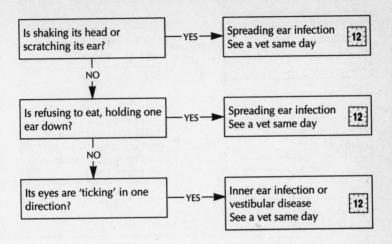

1. Prevent the cat from falling and injuring itself. Avoid bright lights.
2. Look for signs of head injuries that indicate trauma. Get immediate veterinary attention if there are signs of injury or shock. Transport the cat in a dark, enclosed box.
3. Examine the ears for wax, inflammation or discharge – all signs of external ear infection that can move to the inner ear and cause loss of balance. Get veterinary help the same day.

MOUTH INJURIES

A cat should not drool, should not avoid food when it is hungry, should chew, lap water and swallow normally, and show no signs of pain when its jaws are opened or its mouth touched.

Mouth odor should not be repellent.

MOUTH INJURIES

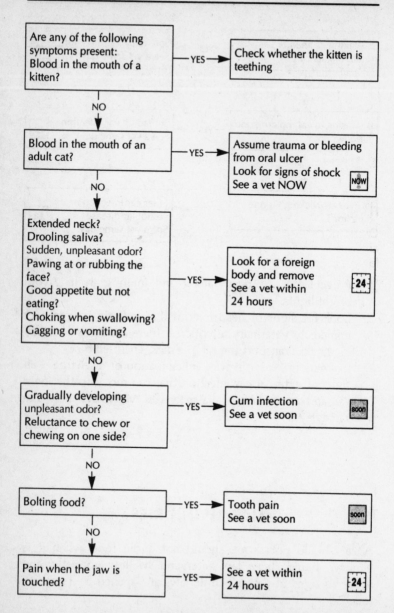

Are any of the following symptoms present:
Blood in the mouth of a kitten? —YES→ Check whether the kitten is teething

NO

Blood in the mouth of an adult cat? —YES→ Assume trauma or bleeding from oral ulcer
Look for signs of shock
See a vet NOW [NOW]

NO

Extended neck?
Drooling saliva?
Sudden, unpleasant odor?
Pawing at or rubbing the face?
Good appetite but not eating?
Choking when swallowing?
Gagging or vomiting? —YES→ Look for a foreign body and remove
See a vet within 24 hours [24]

NO

Gradually developing unpleasant odor?
Reluctance to chew or chewing on one side? —YES→ Gum infection
See a vet soon [soon]

NO

Bolting food? —YES→ Tooth pain
See a vet soon [soon]

NO

Pain when the jaw is touched? —YES→ See a vet within 24 hours [24]

WATCH FOR SHOCK

Pale or white gums, rapid breathing, weak and rapid pulse, cold extremities, general weakness.

(For treatment of shock see under **Shock** on page 10.)

---

1. In good light, open the mouth and examine the teeth and hard palate.

Fig. 1: Open the mouth

Check for the site of bleeding and for any foreign objects lodged between the teeth or against the hard palate.

2. Apply a cold compress to any accessible bleeding site. Look for signs of shock.
3. Using a blunt object or the handle of a teaspoon, loosen and remove pieces of bone that are lodged between the teeth or against the hard palate.

Fig. 2: Remove the irritating object

The blunt object acts as a lever to pry the foreign object from where it is stuck.

127

4. If the mouth is burned (by electricity or caustic chemical), place the cat on its side with its neck on a folded towel and its nose down.
5. Lift the lip to expose the gums and flush the mouth for at least five minutes with cold running water.

*   **Do not tilt the head back to stop bleeding**
*   **Avoid stroking around the head and mouth when there is discomfort in the mouth**

NOSE INJURIES

Observe the type of discharge from the nose and whether it is from one or both nostrils. Bleeding is almost always a result of serious and potentially life threatening trauma.

WATCH FOR SHOCK

Pale or white gums, rapid breathing, weak and rapid pulse, cold extremities, general weakness.

(For treatment of shock see under **Shock** on page 10.)

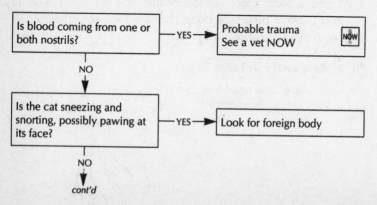

Is blood coming from one or both nostrils? ──YES──▶ Probable trauma See a vet NOW

NO

Is the cat sneezing and snorting, possibly pawing at its face? ──YES──▶ Look for foreign body

NO

cont'd

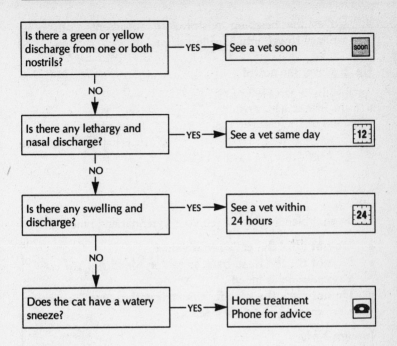

Is there a green or yellow discharge from one or both nostrils?	—YES→	See a vet soon

NO ↓

Is there any lethargy and nasal discharge?	—YES→	See a vet same day

NO ↓

Is there any swelling and discharge?	—YES→	See a vet within 24 hours

NO ↓

Does the cat have a watery sneeze?	—YES→	Home treatment Phone for advice

Nosebleed:

1. Keep the cat quiet and confined.
2. Examine quickly for signs of shock.
3. Apply a cold compress (cold cloth) to the top of the nose between the eyes and nostrils.

Fig. 1: Apply a cold compress

Bleeding should stop within four minutes.

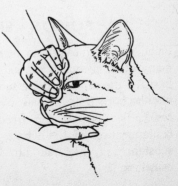

4. Cover the bleeding nostril with absorbent cloth or a sanitary towel until bleeding stops.

Fig. 2: Cover the nostril

An absorbent pad allows a clot to form. Bleeding may recur when this clot is removed.

5. Even if bleeding stops, see your veterinarian immediately.

- **Do not hold the cat's mouth shut**
- **Do not tilt the head back to lessen bleeding.** The cat may choke on its blood
- **Do not pack the bleeding nostril with gauze.** This may cause sneezing and more bleeding

Foreign body:

1. If you can see the foreign object in the nose carefully remove it with tweezers.
2. If you cannot see the foreign object or cannot remove it, take your cat to your veterinarian the same day. (The most likely foreign body is a blade of grass or similar plant material.)

POISON – SKIN CONTACT

Paint, paint remover, tar, petroleum products, motor oil and many other chemicals can all cause irritating skin damage and burns. If the cat licks these substances, the inside of the mouth may be burned. If they are swallowed, general poisoning may result. Because of their freedom to roam, cats may suffer contamination of the whole body by poisons or corrosive substances if they fall into liquids such as paint stripping caustic soda.

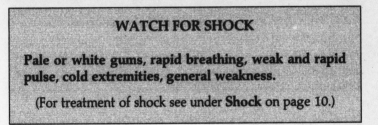

WATCH FOR SHOCK

Pale or white gums, rapid breathing, weak and rapid pulse, cold extremities, general weakness.

(For treatment of shock see under **Shock** on page 10.)

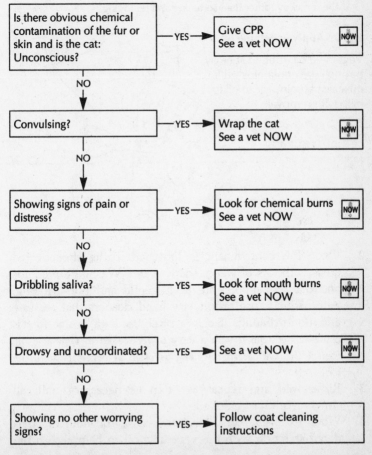

Is there obvious chemical contamination of the fur or skin and is the cat: Unconscious? —YES→ Give CPR / See a vet NOW [NOW]

NO

Convulsing? —YES→ Wrap the cat / See a vet NOW [NOW]

NO

Showing signs of pain or distress? —YES→ Look for chemical burns / See a vet NOW [NOW]

NO

Dribbling saliva? —YES→ Look for mouth burns / See a vet NOW [NOW]

NO

Drowsy and uncoordinated? —YES→ See a vet NOW [NOW]

NO

Showing no other worrying signs? —YES→ Follow coat cleaning instructions

If the cat's coat is contaminated with paint, tar or motor oil:

Do not use paint stripper, paint brush cleaner, paint thinner, turpentine, turpentine substitute or mineral spirits. Do not use concentrated biological detergents.

1. Wearing rubber gloves, rub large amounts of vegetable or mineral oil into the contaminated areas to loosen the substance. (If the contaminating substance has hardened solid, cut the fur away rather than softening and removing.)

Fig. 1: Apply vegetable oil

Vegetable oil, rubbed liberally through the contaminated fur, mixes with paint, tar or oil to help with removal.

2. Once the contaminant is loosened, bathe the affected areas with lots of warm, soapy water. Washing-up liquids and baby shampoos are both gentle and non-irritating. Alternatively, use proprietary hand cleaners that are safe and non-irritating. If only a small area such as one foot is contaminated, rub it with a terry towel soaked in vegetable oil. Repeat this with fresh towelling as often as necessary until the foot is clean.

3. Rinse well and repeat as often as necessary until all contamination is removed.

4. When extensive contamination occurs, rub flour or powdered starch in with the vegetable oil to help absorb the

poison. Remove the mixture with a wide-toothed comb then bathe the fur in soapy detergent and rinse thoroughly.

If the cat's coat is contaminated by anything other than paint, tar, petroleum products and motor oil:
1. Flush the contaminated area for at least five minutes with large quantities of clean water.
2. If the whole body has been contaminated with alkali such as caustic soda, flush for at least fifteen minutes. Concentrate on the eyes. Make sure that the armpits and groin receive as much water as other parts of the body. See **Eye injuries** on page 106.
3. Wearing gloves, wash the affected areas with warm, soapy water, mild detergent such as baby shampoo or washing-up liquid.

POISON – INHALED

Inhaled poisons most often interfere with breathing. Others, concentrated insecticide fumes for example, may cause neurological signs like twitching and salivating. If smoke or irritants such as tear gas have been inhaled, assume that the air passages will be inflamed.

Do not put yourself at risk by entering an environment containing dangerous toxic fumes.

WATCH FOR SHOCK

Pale or white gums, rapid breathing, weak and rapid pulse, cold extremities, general weakness.

(For treatment of shock see under **Shock** on page 10.)

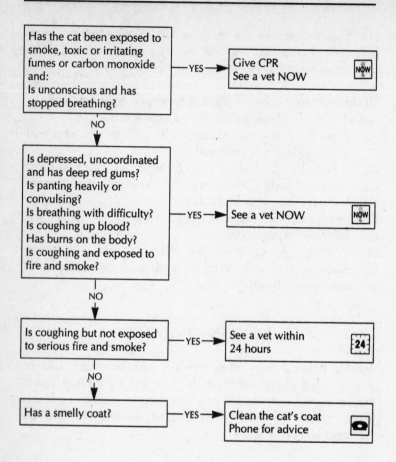

Has the cat been exposed to smoke, toxic or irritating fumes or carbon monoxide and:
Is unconscious and has stopped breathing? — YES → Give CPR / See a vet NOW

Is depressed, uncoordinated and has deep red gums?
Is panting heavily or convulsing?
Is breathing with difficulty?
Is coughing up blood?
Has burns on the body?
Is coughing and exposed to fire and smoke? — YES → See a vet NOW

Is coughing but not exposed to serious fire and smoke? — YES → See a vet within 24 hours

Has a smelly coat? — YES → Clean the cat's coat / Phone for advice

1. For all inhaled poisons, keep the cat's airway open, maintain breathing and assist circulation by giving CPR when necessary.
2. If the cat is convulsing, wrap it loosely in a light towel.
3. Get immediate veterinary help.
4. If there is time to do so, flush the cat's eyes with lots of fresh water or proprietary eyewash.

Do not underestimate the damage caused by inhaling smoke or other irritant fumes. Serious and potentially fatal swelling may affect the air passages hours later. After any serious inhalation accident always get veterinary advice and assistance.

POISON – SWALLOWED

Cats are very sensible about what they eat. A fortunate consequence is that accidental poisoning is rare. Cats are most likely to be poisoned accidentally by overzealous application of flea killing insecticides or by being given aspirin, a dangerous drug for cats, to relieve pain. Cats poison themselves by licking toxic or burning chemicals off their coats. Unfortunately they may also suffer from malicious poisoning.

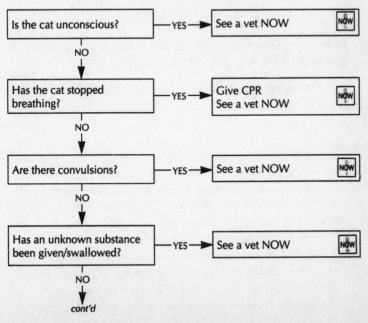

Is the cat unconscious?	—YES→	See a vet NOW

NO ↓

Has the cat stopped breathing?	—YES→	Give CPR See a vet NOW

NO ↓

Are there convulsions?	—YES→	See a vet NOW

NO ↓

Has an unknown substance been given/swallowed?	—YES→	See a vet NOW

NO ↓

cont'd

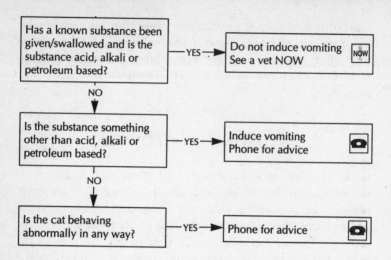

Has a known substance been given/swallowed and is the substance acid, alkali or petroleum based? —YES→ Do not induce vomiting See a vet NOW

NO

Is the substance something other than acid, alkali or petroleum based? —YES→ Induce vomiting Phone for advice

NO

Is the cat behaving abnormally in any way? —YES→ Phone for advice

WATCH FOR SHOCK

Pale or white gums, rapid breathing, weak and rapid pulse, cold extremities, general weakness.

(For treatment of shock see under **Shock** on page 10.)

1. Do not panic. If shock has developed or the cat is unconscious, keep the airway open, maintain breathing and circulation and see your veterinarian immediately.

2. If convulsions have developed, prevent the cat from damaging itself or from biting you and others and get immediate veterinary help.

3. If poison has been swallowed in the last two hours (but not acid, alkali and petroleum based poisons), induce vomiting by giving a large crystal of washing soda, concentrated salt or 3% hydrogen peroxide solution, one

teaspoon every fifteen minutes until vomiting occurs. Inducing vomiting is only effective if the poison has been swallowed within four hours. (Only give washing soda or other emetics if the cat is conscious and alert.)

The following household items are acids, alkalis or petroleum products:

- Caustic soda
- Chlorine bleach
- Dishwasher granules
- Drain cleaner
- Kerosene
- Laundry detergents
- Lye
- Oven cleaner
- Paint stripper and remover
- Paint thinner
- Petrol
- Polishes – furniture, floor and shoe
- Toilet cleaner
- Wood preservatives

Fig. 1: Open the cat's mouth and insert washing soda

One hand lifts the upper jaw, squeezing the upper lips over the teeth. The other hand drops the washing soda crystal or ball of salt to the back of the throat.

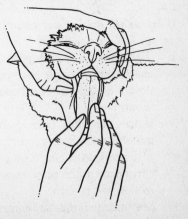

Fig. 2: Hold the mouth shut

One hand keeps the cat's mouth shut. The other strokes the neck. When the cat licks its lips it has swallowed the emetic. Vomiting occurs within several minutes.

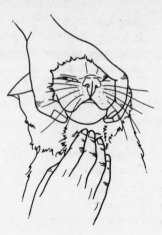

4. Give one to two teaspoons of a slurry of activated charcoal in water. (This helps absorb any remaining poison.)
5. If the poison is unknown, do not throw out the vomit. Keep a sample to take to your veterinarian. See your veterinarian as soon as possible.
6. If the poison is known, telephone your veterinarian or poison control center for advice.
7. If any signs of poisoning develop, give first aid and transport the cat to the veterinarian as soon as possible.

If an alkali, acid or petroleum based poison is swallowed, do not induce vomiting:

1. If the poison is acid, give egg white, bicarbonate of soda, charcoal powder or olive oil by mouth.
2. Apply a paste of bicarbonate of soda to any burns in the mouth.
3. If the skin has been burned, flush for at least fifteen minutes with clean running water.
4. If the poison is alkali, give egg white or small amounts of citrus fruit juice or vinegar. Pour vinegar on alkali burns to skin and mouth.
5. See your veterinarian immediately.

SPECIFIC POISONS

Household cleaners – drain cleaner, solvents, paint stripper, all products with alkali or acid symbol on labels
Poisoning most frequently occurs when these substances are wrongly used to clean the cat's fur. The cat swallows the substance while cleaning itself.

Look for:
- Inflamed skin
- Vomiting
- Diarrhea
- Possible convulsions
- Depression
- Coughing
- Abdominal pain
- Redness in the mouth and on the tongue

1. Do not induce vomiting.
2. Give one tablespoon of olive oil or similar vegetable oil orally.
3. Wash the skin and coat thoroughly with soapy water. (Wear rubber gloves to avoid burning your own skin. See **Poison – skin contact**, page 130.)
4. Get immediate veterinary help.

Insecticides – flea collars, concentrated washes, shampoos, sprays containing organophosphates and carbamates
Poisoning occurs most commonly when a cat licks insecticide off its coat.

Look for:
Carbamates:
- Agitation
- Restlessness
- Twitching
- Salivation
- Convulsions
- Coma

ORGANOPHOSPHATES:

- Hind leg weaknesses
- Breathing difficulties
- Muscle tremors
- Salivation
- Increased urinating/ defecating

1. Provide first aid according to the needs of the cat.
2. If consumed, induce vomiting and give activated charcoal.
3. If there is skin contact, wash off remaining insecticide with soapy water. (Wear rubber gloves to protect yourself from exposure.)
4. Get immediate veterinary help. (An antidote is available from your veterinarian.)

Rodent poison

Many different types of rodenticide are available. Check the packaging to find out the chemical name of the poison. The cat is usually poisoned by eating the poisoned rodent.

Warfarin
Look for:

- Vomiting
- Lethargy
- Signs of internal bleeding
- Pale gums and signs of shock
- Bruising to the skin

1. If the cat has just eaten a poisoned rodent, induce vomiting then give activated charcoal by mouth.
2. If the cat shows signs of poisoning, keep the cat warm, treat for shock and take the cat and a sample of the rodenticide or the packaging to the veterinarian as soon as possible.

   (Vitamin K, given by injection, is a specific antidote for warfarin poisoning.)
3. Warfarin poisoning may be fatal.

Strychnine
Look for:
- A worried look
- Tenseness and stiffness leading to convulsions

Can be fatal within an hour.

1. Induce vomiting only if breathing is regular and give activated charcoal.
2. Get immediate veterinary help.

Sodium fluoroacetate
Look for:
- Initial excitement followed by depression
- Convulsions
- Vomiting
- Urinating and repeated bowel motions

1. Induce vomiting and give activated charcoal by mouth.
2. Keep the cat warm.
3. Get immediate veterinary help.

Slug and snail bait – metaldehyde

Cats are occasionally maliciously poisoned by meat laced with metaldehyde. Under normal circumstances, cats are unlikely to eat the poison on its own.

Look for:
- Tremors
- Salivation
- Convulsions
- Coma

1. If recently swallowed, induce vomiting with soda crystals, 3% hydrogen peroxide or a ball of salt.
2. See your veterinarian as soon as possible. (Treatment may involve prolonged anaesthesia.)

Acetominophen (Tylenol)

Poisoning occurs most commonly as a result of the cat being given this popular painkiller to relieve pain. It is lethal to cats. As little as half an adult tablet or capsule of acetominophen can kill an adult cat. Do not give this drug to cats.

Look for:
- Lethargy
- A bluish discoloration to the lips
- Puffy, swollen head and face

1. Induce vomiting with washing soda crystals or 3% hydrogen peroxide.
2. Give no other medicines.
3. Get immediate veterinary help. If this is not possible, give 250 mg of vitamin C by mouth immediately.

Antifreeze – ethylene glycol

Some cats enjoy the taste of antifreeze that has leaked from car radiators. Newer types of antifreeze are not toxic. Ethylene glycol poisoning can be fatal.

Look for:
- Wobbling
- Convulsions
- Vomiting
- Collapse
- Coma

1. If recently swallowed, induce vomiting and give activated charcoal by mouth.
2. Get veterinary attention urgently.
3. If veterinary treatment is a great distance away, give small amounts of alcohol by mouth. (This reduces ethylene glycol damage to the kidneys.)

Aspirin

Poisoning occurs most commonly as a result of the cat being given aspirin to relieve pain. Do not give aspirin to cats. It takes almost four days for the drug to be cleared from the body. Even with small doses, overdosage is likely.

Look for:
- Poor appetite
- Depression
- Abdominal cramp
- Vomiting with or without blood
- Uncoordination

1. Induce vomiting with washing soda crystals. (This also counteracts the poisoning effect of aspirin.)
2. Give no other medicines.
3. Telephone your veterinarian for further advice.

Illicit drugs

Cats either find illicit drugs such as cannabis or ecstasy accidentally or are sometimes given them.

Look for:
- Uncoordination
- Agitation
- Fear biting
- Dilated pupils

1. Avoid any unnecessary sensory stimulation such as light and sound.
2. Get immediate veterinary attention.

Sedatives, antidepressants and antianxiety drugs

These prescription medicines may be intentionally given to the cat and cause poisoning. Drugs called tricyclic antidepressants may cause fatal heart arrythmias in cats.

Look for:
- Depression
- Staggering
- Restlessness or agitation
- Erratic heartbeat
- Deep sleep or coma

1. If the cat has just been given the pills, induce vomiting with a washing soda crystal, 3% hydrogen peroxide or a ball of salt. Feed activated charcoal.
2. Keep the cat warm. Talk to it constantly.
3. Give first aid if the cat is slipping into a coma.
4. Telephone your veterinarian for advice.

Prevent poisoning:

- Do not give any prescription or proprietary human medicines to cats without first getting your veterinarian's approval
- Keep all cleaners, garden and do-it-yourself chemicals out of the reach of cats and where they cannot be knocked down
- Keep all insecticides and petroleum products out of the reach of cats and where they cannot be knocked down
- When using poisons for weeds, insects or rodents, ensure your cat and other pets cannot get into the areas in which poison has been laid or applied. Follow strictly the instructions on the packet
- When using insecticides directly on a cat, follow strictly the instructions on the packet. Prevent the cat from licking the insecticide off its coat
- Ensure that all medicines, both human and animal, are kept in their original containers and are labelled correctly, including the number of pills originally prescribed. This information will be valuable in case of an accidental overdose

POISONOUS PLANTS

Reduce the risk of accidental poisoning. Prevent your cat from playfully chewing on or eating any of the following plants, flowers or fungi:

- Amaryllis (*Amaryllis*)
- Autumn crocus (*Colochicum autumnale*)
- Bleeding heart (*Dicentra spectabilis*)
- Bloodroot (*Sanguinaria canadensis*)
- Caster oil plant (*Ricinus communis*) (Very dangerous)
- Dumbcane (*Dieffenbachia*) (Very dangerous)
- Flower bulbs of any kind
- Foxglove (*Digitalis purpurea*)
- Jerusalem cherry (*Solanum pseudocapsicum*)
- Larkspur (*Delphinium*)
- Lily of the valley (*Convallaria majalis*)
- Mistletoe (*Viscum album*) (Very poisonous)
- Mushrooms – any wild fungi you cannot safely identify
- Rhubarb (*Rheum rhaponticum*)
- Stinging nettles (*Urtica dioica*)
- Thorn apple or jimsonweed (*Datura stramonium*) (Very dangerous)
- Virginia creeper (*Parthenocissus quinquefolia*)

Do not let your cat chew on leaves, wood or branches from any of these trees or shrubs:

- Azalea
- Box
- Cherry laurel (Very dangerous)
- Chinaberry tree
- Hemlock (Very dangerous)
- Horsechestnut
- Ivy (leaves and berries) (Very dangerous)
- Laburnum

- Oleander (Very dangerous)
- Privet
- Rhododendron
- Wisteria
- Yew (Very dangerous)

PUNCTURE WOUNDS

Puncture wounds to the skin are almost always infected. Bites from other cats are the most common puncture wounds. They may leave little superficial damage, no more than a matt of hair where the tooth has penetrated, but under the skin pus builds up as an abscess. This infection can spread to other parts of the body causing serious illness.

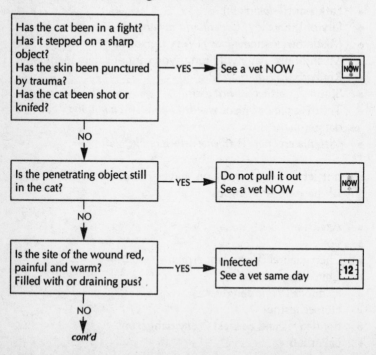

cont'd

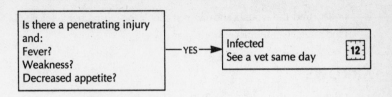

Is there a penetrating injury and: Fever? Weakness? Decreased appetite?	→ YES →	Infected See a vet same day 12

ANIMAL BITES AND ABSCESSES

1. Calm the cat. Restrain it and muzzle if necessary. Do not put yourself at risk. The cat might bite and scratch if it is still excited or in pain.
2. If the chest is punctured, cover the wound with a clean, damp cloth. Bandage the chest tightly enough to seal the wound.
3. Monitor shock, give CPR as necessary and get immediate veterinary attention.
4. If the abdomen is punctured and internal organs exposed, immediately wash them off with clean water when possible, wrap the cat's abdomen with a warm, damp sheet, keep the cat warm and get urgent veterinary assistance.
5. If muscle is punctured, clean the wounds with 3% hydrogen peroxide, keep the cat warm, monitor for signs of shock and get immediate veterinary help.

Do not use any antiseptics or disinfectants on open chest or abdomen puncture wounds.

Bites to the feet cause swelling, lameness and behavior changes. (See **Bites and Stings** on page 67.)

GUNSHOT WOUNDS

1. Calm the cat and restrain it if necessary.
2. Treat obvious emergencies such as bleeding.
3. Even if the cat appears only slightly injured, get immediate veterinary assistance. (Air rifle injuries are deceptive. The fur is

pulled into the wound and hides it. Look for hiding behavior and tenderness. Get immediate veterinary help.)

ARROWS

1. Do not pull the arrow out.
2. Cut the arrow about 5 cm (2 inches) from the cat's body.

Fig. 1: Cut the arrow

The arrow is cut near the cat's body. This reduces further damage when the cat is moved.

3. Bandage tightly around the arrow's point of entry. (This minimizes movement of the arrow and prevents further internal damage.)
4. Treat shock as necessary and get immediate veterinary attention.

PORCUPINE QUILLS

1. When possible, get immediate veterinary attention. The quills will be removed under anaesthesia.
2. If only a few quills are embedded, use long nosed pliers to pull out each quill following the angle of the quill shaft.

SPLINTERS

1. Wash off dirt and debris from the skin with soap and warm water.
2. Grasp the splinter with tweezers and remove it.

3. Once the splinter is removed wash the area again with warm, soapy water or 3% hydrogen peroxide.

Do not bandage puncture wounds unless they are bleeding profusely, are in the chest or the penetrating object is still lodged in the wound.

After any penetrating injury always contact your veterinarian. Although tetanus is much less common in cats than it is in humans, this bacterium thrives in deep wounds. Your veterinarian may want to give tetanus antitoxin.

Tetanus develops five to fifteen days after a penetrating injury. The signs are:

- Sensitivity to light and sound
- Ears stiffer than normal
- General stiffness leading to paralysis
- Inability to stand

SCRATCHING

Sudden, intense scratching occurs during allergic reactions. Often called hives, the allergic reaction sometimes leads to dangerous anaphylactic shock. Uncontrolled scratching for other less serious reasons can lead to severe self-inflicted injuries.

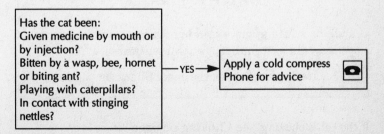

Has the cat been:
Given medicine by mouth or by injection?
Bitten by a wasp, bee, hornet or biting ant?
Playing with caterpillars?
In contact with stinging nettles?

→ YES →

Apply a cold compress
Phone for advice

1. Restrain the cat.
2. Examine the skin and apply cold compresses for fifteen minutes to the most itchy regions.
3. Try to identify and eliminate the cause of itchiness.
4. If scratching continues or gets worse, make an appointment to see your veterinarian.

Avoid problems:

- When possible, try to prevent your cat from playing with irritating or biting insects
- If a new flea collar is put on the cat, watch carefully for the first few days for signs of local irritation

SWALLOWED OBJECTS

Kittens and inquisitive adult cats may swallow indigestible articles, especially items attached to thread. Some objects are small enough to pass through the stomach and intestines, while others may start the journey but then get stuck. Sometimes, objects remain in the stomach.

WATCH FOR SHOCK

Pale or white gums, rapid breathing, weak and rapid pulse, cold extremities, general weakness.

(For treatment of shock see under **Shock** on page 10.)

If the cat is choking, see **Choking** on page 90.

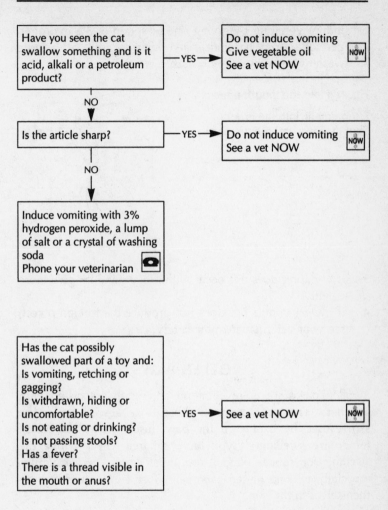

Have you seen the cat swallow something and is it acid, alkali or a petroleum product? —YES→ Do not induce vomiting / Give vegetable oil / See a vet NOW

NO

Is the article sharp? —YES→ Do not induce vomiting / See a vet NOW

NO

Induce vomiting with 3% hydrogen peroxide, a lump of salt or a crystal of washing soda / Phone your veterinarian

Has the cat possibly swallowed part of a toy and: / Is vomiting, retching or gagging? / Is withdrawn, hiding or uncomfortable? / Is not eating or drinking? / Is not passing stools? / Has a fever? / There is a thread visible in the mouth or anus? —YES→ See a vet NOW

1. If the article is still in the mouth, remove it if possible. Do not pull on thread, string or tinsel hanging from the mouth or anus. Do not cut it short. Get immediate veterinary help.

2. If the object is not alkali, acid, petroleum product or sharp,

induce vomiting by giving one teaspoon of 3% hydrogen peroxide or a hazelnut sized lump of salt or a large washing soda crystal by mouth.

Fig. 1: Hold the mouth open

Drop emetic into the mouth.
Shut the jaws and rub the neck.

3. If vomiting does not occur within five minutes, give more emetic.
4. If the cat vomits but does not produce the foreign object, see your veterinarian immediately.

SWOLLEN PAWS

Swollen paws are quite common and often associated with lameness. The most common cause is an abscess under the skin caused by a bite on the paw. Insect stings also cause temporary swelling. If you have children, check above the swelling for rubber bands. You must search very carefully, especially in long haired cats, as rubber bands quickly bury themselves in the skin.

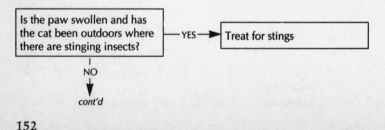

Is the paw swollen and has the cat been outdoors where there are stinging insects? — YES ▶ Treat for stings

NO
cont'd

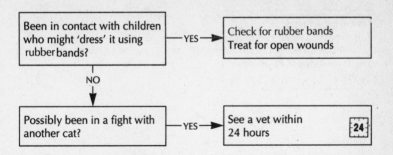

Been in contact with children who might 'dress' it using rubber bands? —YES→ Check for rubber bands / Treat for open wounds

NO ↓

Possibly been in a fight with another cat? —YES→ See a vet within 24 hours

Insect stings are more common in young, playful cats. Rubber bands are most often put on a cat's legs but cats can also accidentally put them on themselves, especially when playing with rubber bands and catching them in their teeth.

URINARY PROBLEMS

Anatomically, male cats are more prone to urinary tract blockages than females. A plug of material blocks urine flow from the urinary bladder to the outside. If not treated, this may lead to shock and death.

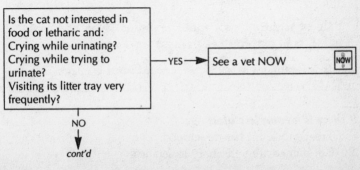

Is the cat not interested in food or letharic and: Crying while urinating? Crying while trying to urinate? Visiting its litter tray very frequently? —YES→ See a vet NOW

NO ↓

cont'd

153

URINARY PROBLEMS

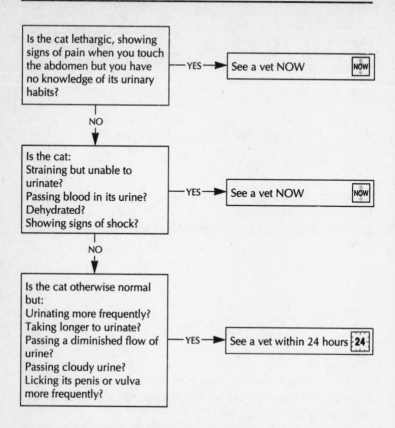

Is the cat lethargic, showing signs of pain when you touch the abdomen but you have no knowledge of its urinary habits? —YES→ See a vet NOW **NOW**

NO

Is the cat:
Straining but unable to urinate?
Passing blood in its urine?
Dehydrated?
Showing signs of shock? —YES→ See a vet NOW **NOW**

NO

Is the cat otherwise normal but:
Urinating more frequently?
Taking longer to urinate?
Passing a diminished flow of urine?
Passing cloudy urine?
Licking its penis or vulva more frequently? —YES→ See a vet within 24 hours **24**

WATCH FOR SHOCK

Pale or white gums, rapid breathing, weak and rapid pulse, cold extremities, general weakness.

(For treatment of shock see under **Shock** on page 10.)

If there is a complete blockage:
1. Treat shock if it has developed.
2. Get immediate veterinary assistance.

154

3. If any urine has been passed, try to collect a sample to help your veterinarian make an accurate diagnosis of the cause of the blockage.

If the cat is passing urine with difficulty:
1. Collect a urine sample in a clean container.
2. See your veterinarian within twenty-four hours.

VOMITING

Dribbling, lip licking and excessive swallowing are often signs of nausea and impending vomiting. Cats readily vomit to empty their stomachs of hairballs. More serious vomiting accompanies a wide range of serious conditions.

WATCH FOR SHOCK

Pale or white gums, rapid breathing, weak and rapid pulse, cold extremities, general weakness.

(For treatment of shock see under **Shock** on page 10.)

If vomiting is accompanied by diarrhea, see **Diarrhea** on page 100.

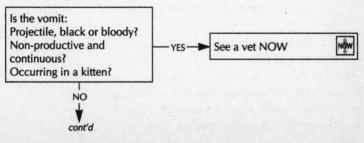

Is the vomit:
Projectile, black or bloody?
Non-productive and continuous?
Occurring in a kitten?

— YES → See a vet NOW

NO
↓
cont'd

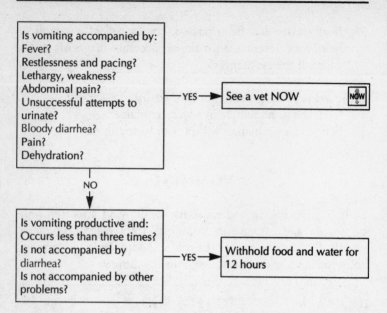

Is vomiting accompanied by:
Fever?
Restlessness and pacing?
Lethargy, weakness?
Abdominal pain?
Unsuccessful attempts to urinate?
Bloody diarrhea?
Pain?
Dehydration?

— YES → See a vet NOW

NO ↓

Is vomiting productive and:
Occurs less than three times?
Is not accompanied by diarrhea?
Is not accompanied by other problems?

— YES → Withhold food and water for 12 hours

1. Take away all food and water.
2. If the cat is dehydrated or in shock, treat shock and get immediate veterinary help.
3. If the cat is not dehydrated or in shock, withhold water for twelve hours and food for twelve to twenty-four hours.
4. Offer an ice cube or one teaspoon of soda water every few hours to moisten the mouth.
5. After twelve to twenty-four hours offer one to three teaspoons of bland food (chicken or meaty baby food). If this is not vomited, offer a little more every one to two hours.
6. Return to the regular diet the next day.

Avoid problems:
- Groom your cat regularly to get rid of excess hair
- Do not change the cat's diet abruptly
- Do not let your cat scavenge

PART FOUR

PREVENTING EMERGENCIES

How to Reduce the Risk of Emergencies

Reduce the risk of emergencies happening by taking simple precautions:

- Control your cat

  It is a jungle out there. Free access to the outdoors is exciting but also extremely dangerous. Free roaming cats run high risks of serious trauma. There are dangers indoors too, especially falling from balconies and open windows. Do not believe that cats are always sensible, they are not. So-called 'high-rise syndrome', cats falling from great heights, is a common emergency.

- Prevent scavenging

  Secure refuse both inside your home and on your property with tight lids.

- Arrange for a yearly medical examination and booster inoculation

  Prevention or early diagnosis of conditions is almost always physically and financially less costly than emergency treatment.

- Control internal and external parasites

  Parasites spread disease. Worm your cat routinely and control seasonal parasites with appropriate inhibitors and insecticides.

- Neuter your cat

  Discuss neutering with your veterinarian. Neutered cats are less likely to roam and enjoy reduced risk of several serious medical conditions.

- Provide routine hygienic care for the skin and coat, teeth and gums, nails and anal glands

  Emergencies are less likely to occur if you carry out routine cat 'maintenance'.

- Avoid hazardous household situations

  Keep all household chemicals, cleaners, medicines or dangerous plants out of your cat's reach and in places where they will not fall down. If your cat is a chewer, hide away all electrical cords. Always check that your cat is not in your clothes dryer before turning it on. Get into the habit of banging on the bonnet of your car before starting up the engine. (In cold weather cats are attracted to the heat in the engine block. Ask your neighbors to do the same.)

- Avoid hazards when the cat is traveling with you

  Never leave a cat in a car on a warm day.

IDENTIFICATION

Identification is essential in case your cat gets lost. Do not take chances. Permanent identification with tattoos and microchips offers more security than name tags worn on collars.

TATTOOS

Consider tattooing if there is a standardized identification system where you live. While the cat is sedated a registered number is tattooed inside the ear. Always report your change of address or telephone number to the registering authority.

MICROCHIPS

Consider having an identification microchip implanted under your cat's skin if the cat shelters in your area routinely scan cats that arrive at the shelters for identifying microchips. The inert microchip contains information that is 'read' when the chip is scanned by a reader. It is inserted by an 'injection' between the shoulders. Always report your change of address or telephone number to the registering authority. (In Europe, all microchips are standardized and readable by different readers.)

ENGRAVED NAME TAGS

Have your cat's name and your telephone number engraved on one side of the tag. Consider having the word 'Vet' and your veterinarian's telephone number engraved on the other side. Replace the tag with a new one when you move.

NAME CYLINDERS

Write your cat's name and your telephone number on a piece of paper, place it in the cylinder and screw it shut. Cylinders have a tendency to unscrew. Ensure your cat's does not by painting the tightened cylinder with nail varnish. Change the enclosed information when you move.

COLLARS

Even if your cat does not go outdoors, make sure it wears a collar with accompanying identification. This ensures identification if your cat 'escapes'. If your cat routinely goes outdoors, ensure that the collar has an elastic insert so that it does not get caught on branches when the cat is climbing.

TRAINING AND EXERCISE

TRAINING

If your cat goes outdoors, train it to meow when it hears its name. Tease it with a food it craves and say its name. Give it the food snack when it meows. Repeat this training until the cat reliably meows simply when it hears its name. By training your cat to meow when you call it, it is more likely you will be able to find it outdoors if it is injured or hiding from danger.

EXERCISE

All cats need physical and mental stimulation. Play with your cat when you are at home. Amuse it. Feed it just before you leave, as it is then more likely to sleep while you are out rather than doing the 'wall of death' up your curtains. If your cat is housebound and likes to chew on greens, remove any potentially toxic house plants and provide grass as a healthy substitute. To be extra kind and generous to the feline herbivore, invest in a spider plant. The leaves contain a chemical similar to that in catmint.

VACCINATION

A vaccine stimulates the cat's immune system to build defences against a specific disease. Vaccines are usually made from viruses or bacteria that have been made safe but still stimulate the immune system to create protection. Some vaccines are genetically engineered and contain only the bits of a virus necessary to build immunity. Your veterinarian will advise on what diseases exist in your area and the prevention program most suitable for your cat.

Diseases commonly vaccinated against include:

Leukemia
Leukemia virus is the most common infectious cause of death in cats. This slow-acting virus attacks the cat's natural defences and allows other serious diseases to develop. These include:

- Severe anaemia
- Tumors of lymph nodes
- Severe gum infection
- Kidney failure

Leukemia virus infection can be fatal.

Panleucopenia
The signs of panleucopenia are:
- Vomiting and diarrhea
- Lethargy and listlessness
- Dehydration

Panleucopenia or 'cat distemper' or 'feline enteritis' can be fatal.

Herpes and calici viruses
The signs of these viral infections are:
- Sneezing
- Inflamed and discharging eyes
- Inflamed gums
- Mouth ulcers
- Fever and debility

These viruses can be fatal to young kittens. Once contracted, herpes infection may recur throughout life.

Chlamydia
The signs of Chalmydia infection are:
- Severely inflamed and discharging eyes

This infection is very contagious and needs prolonged antibiotic treatment to cure.

Coronavirus
The signs of this infection vary but the most serious manifestation is called infectious peritonitis (FIP).

The signs of FIP are:
- Swollen abdomen
- Anemia
- Weight loss
- Dehydration

FIP is invariably fatal.

Rabies

Preventative vaccination against rabies is required throughout most of continental Europe and North America. A single vaccination provides protection for between one and three years. Aerial vaccination of foxes throughout both Western and Eastern Europe with genetically engineered anti-rabies vaccine is proving extremely effective in reducing and, in some countries, totally eliminating this disease from wildlife.

PARASITE CONTROL

External parasites such as fleas, ticks, mites and lice cause itching but can also transmit a range of diseases. Internal parasites debilitate cats, increasing the risk of serious conditions developing. Prevent parasites from treating your cat like a mobile restaurant. Follow your veterinarian's advice. Carry out routine parasite prevention measures.

EXTERNAL PARASITES

If your cat has black, shiny dust in its fur or it has itchy, inflamed or dandruffy skin look for fleas. Do not assume there are no parasites if you do not see any. Most itchy skin problems in cats are caused by parasites. Make an appointment for your veterinarian to examine your cat. Prevent parasites from infesting your cat and possibly your family by using insecticides and parasite inhibitors on all your cats and dogs. Always treat your home as well as your cat when fleas are prevalent.

Fleas, mites, lice
Signs of infestation:
- Itching and scratching
- Inflamed skin
- Dull, dandruffy coat
- Lice eggs glued to hair
- Parasites may or may not be visible

Prevention:
- Start flea prevention before the flea season begins
- Do not let your cat share bedding with other animals that have parasites

INTERNAL PARASITES

If your cat has watery or bloody diarrhea, take a stool specimen with you when you visit your veterinarian. Tests can be carried out to determine which internal parasites, if any, are causing the problem.

Roundworm
Signs of infestation:
- Dull coat
- Poor weight gain or weight loss
- Vomiting or diarrhea, sometimes with pink-white worms passed

Prevention:
- Routinely worm kittens from two weeks of age
- Worm pregnant cats
- Worm cats after prolonged treatment with corticosteroids
- In addition, worm all outdoor cats at least twice yearly with medicine recommended by your veterinarian

Tapeworm

Signs of infestation:
- Distended abdomen
- Rice-grain-like egg sacs in fur around anus

Prevention:
- Control fleas on your cat
- Prevent your cat from eating animal carcasses and offal
- Worm your cat with medicine approved by your veterinarian

Coccidia, **Giardia**, **Babesia** and **Toxoplasma** are other internal parasites for which there is no routine prevention. Toxoplasmosis is a potential health hazard to humans, especially to pregnant women. If your cat goes outdoors or is fed raw meat, avoid contact with its feces during pregnancy.

BODY CARE

TEETH AND GUMS

If you feed your cat on commercial cat food, dry or moist, or if you give it food from your own table but do not brush or otherwise massage its gums, it may develop gum inflammation. By the time the cat's breath smells unpleasant there may be irreversible damage to the roots of some teeth. Keep the teeth and gums healthy and prevent infection.

1. Ensure that at least part of the cat's diet requires tearing and chewing. Feed pieces of uncut meat.
2. Brush your cat's teeth weekly, using a soft child's toothbrush. (Do not use standard toothpaste, most cats dislike it. Only use toothpastes formulated specially for cats. Always reward your cat with praise or a hard snack after you brush its teeth.)

3. If your cat's gums bleed when you brush them, they are already inflamed. Make an appointment to see your veterinarian.

Because they are such fastidious eaters, most, but not all cats can clean their teeth by chewing upon and eating bones. From an early age offer your cat bones, but only if it does not bolt down its food like a dog. Giving your cat bones might also be dangerous in households where several cats eat competitively.

CLAWS

Cats scratch furniture and other objects to leave visible markers of their presence. Always provide a cat with an acceptable scratching post. Older cats need their claws cut more frequently. If left unattended, claws may grow round on themselves and puncture the cat's pads.

1. Hold the paw and look for the living pink tissue (the quick) inside the claw.

Fig. 1: Cutting the claws

(a) How to cut a cat's claws

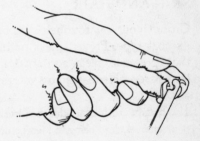

(b) Where to cut a cat's claws

The quick

Where to cut

2. Using purpose made cat nail clippers cut the nail just in front of the quick.
3. If the quick bleeds, apply pressure for two minutes to the cut end of the nail with an absorbent pad.

ANAL GLANDS

If your cat is constantly washing its anal region, or if it is licking its groin or hind legs, it might have blocked anal scent glands.

The signs of blocked glands are:
*   Licking the anal region
*   Licking the groin or hind legs
*   Suddenly jumping up and looking at the hind quarters

Blocked anal glands should be emptied. Your veterinarian can show you how to do this. Preventative emptying reduces the risk of a painful anal abscess forming.

SKIN AND HAIR

Groom your cat routinely according to the specific needs of its coat type. Prevent fleas or treat them at the first sign of their presence. Fleas account for perhaps three out of every four skin problems seen by veterinarians.

1. Brush your cat daily. (Brushing prevents matting but also removes dead hair and loosens dry flaking skin, preventing it from building up. Brushing allows you to examine your cat thoroughly. It should be a pleasure for both you and your cat. Begin daily brushing at a very young age.)
2. Bathe your cat as frequently or infrequently as possible. (Follow your veterinarian's advice. Most cats need to be bathed only for medical reasons. Use shampoos designed for use on cat hair unless advised otherwise.)

3. Do not use dietary supplements in excess. (Sunflower oil and corn oil at a dose of between one teaspoon a day, or proprietary 'GLA' oil supplements may improve a very dry skin if given for at least a month.)

DIET

Good nutrition is essential for good health. Make sure your cat always has access to fresh water. Feed a well balanced diet that is appropriate for your cat's age, condition and energy level.

1. Feed commercial foods only from reputable manufacturers.
2. Ensure that eating exercises your cat's teeth and gums.
3. Serve food at room or body temperature, not directly out of the refrigerator.
4. Discard any dry food not eaten in twenty-four hours.
5. Discard any moist food not eaten in one hour.
6. Make sure a bowl of fresh water is always available.

- Do not feed cats with dog food. (It may be deficient in trace minerals)
- Never feed food that is stale or spoiled
- Only feed bones to cats that chew their food well
- Do not let your cat get overweight

WEIGHT WATCHING

Carrying excess weight does not appear to be as great a health hazard in cats as it is in dogs or in people. Slim cats, however, are more dexterous and less likely to injure themselves.

You should be able to feel your cat's ribs. If you cannot, your cat is probably overweight. Most cats like to nibble.

Reduce calories, not the frequency of meals. Feeding a fat cat a calorie reduced diet, little and often, satisfies the cat's desire to eat constantly.

NEUTERING

Neutering does not make a cat less playful. What it does do is make sex a less important item on the cat's agenda. The bonus for us is that neutered cats are often more human orientated and more playful. When sex is less important, accidents are less likely. As an added benefit females are less likely to develop mammary tumors and males do not carry with them the distinctive, pungent male urine aroma.

The advantages of neutering male cats include:
- Fewer territorial fights
- Less roaming (After neutering cats roam over a smaller territory closer to home)
- Less urine spraying
- No unpleasant tom cat urine smell
- Easier to train
- No fathering of unwanted litters

The disadvantages of neutering male cats include:
- Inability to father litters in the future
- A tendency to gain weight (Weight gain is experienced by ten per cent of cats after they are neutered. Excess weight is readily controlled by adjusting the cat's diet)

The advantages of neutering female cats include:
- No unwanted pregnancies
- No seasonal heat cycles and caterwauling
- No seasonal hormonally induced mood changes
- Less risk of mammary tumors (The risk drops to zero if the female is neutered before her first season)

- No risk of life threatening womb infection (pyometra) later in life (Pyometra is a common emergency in older females. Immediate surgery to remove the pus filled womb is necessary)

The disadvantages of neutering female cats include:
- Inability to have kittens
- A tendency to gain weight (Weight gain is experienced by ten per cent of cats after they are neutered. Excess weight is readily controlled by adjusting the cat's diet)

HOW TO GIVE ORAL MEDICINES

Few cats accept being forced to swallow medicines willingly. Be firm but gentle. Always reward your cat afterwards with soothing words and strokes. When possible, hide the medicine or associate it with something the cat finds enjoyable.

Pills:
1. Calm the cat by speaking to it soothingly. Wrap it gently in a towel to prevent it scratching or escaping.
2. With your forefinger and thumb just behind the canine teeth, draw the jaw up and the upper lips down.
3. Tilt the cat's head back.
4. With the pill in your other hand, draw the lower jaw down and drop or place the pill as far back over the tongue as possible.

Fig. 1: Drop or place the pill in the mouth

Hold the head up to reduce the risk of the pill being spat out.

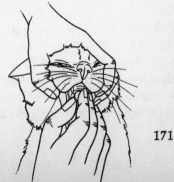

171

5. Immediately close the cat's mouth and rub its throat until you see the cat swallow. Blowing into the nostrils while holding the mouth closed often prompts swallowing.

Fig. 2: Rub the throat

This stimulates swallowing.

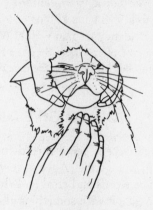

6. Open the mouth to make sure the pill has been swallowed. If it has, praise the cat. If not, repeat the exercise.

Liquid medicines:

1. Hold the upper jaw as you would when giving a pill.
2. Keep the head level. Do not tilt it back as you would when giving a pill.
3. Tip or squirt the medicine into the side of the mouth. Do not squirt it into the back of the mouth, it might go down the windpipe.
4. Close the mouth and rub the throat until the cat swallows.
5. Praise the cat.

Whenever possible, hide pills in food such as a ball of meat. Alternatively, if the pill is tasteless, powder it and mix it in with the cat's food. Hide liquid medicines by mixing them thoroughly into a favorite food. Some medicines should not be given with certain types of food. Always check with your veterinarian before hiding medicine in food.

Some cats are extremely difficult to give oral medicines to. It is important to give a full course of prescribed medicine. If you have difficulties, contact your veterinarian. If you are severely scratched or bitten, always seek medical advice.

HOW TO GIVE EYE MEDICINES

Make certain that eye drops, lotions or ointments, but not their containers, come into direct contact with the eye itself.

Eye ointment:
1. Speak calmly to the cat. Put the cat on a table and wrap it in a towel if necessary.
2. Clean away any eye discharge with a piece of cotton wool dampened with tepid or warm water.
3. With the thumb of one hand, draw the lower lid down. (This forms a space for the ointment.)
4. Support the other hand holding the eye ointment against the cat's head. (This prevents the ointment container from hitting the eye if the cat moves abruptly.)
5. Squeeze a line of ointment in the space formed between the lower lid and the eyeball. (Ointment runs more smoothly if the tube is first warmed in your hands.)
6. Close the eye. (This spreads the ointment evenly over the eye and throughout the socket. Cold ointments often appear grey/white but with body heat become clear within minutes.)
7. Praise the cat and give it a food reward.

Eye drops:
1. Follow the above instructions but do not draw the lower lid away.
2. Squeeze an eye drop on to the upper part of the eye.

Always take care that the medicine container does not come into contact with the eye.

HOW TO GIVE EAR MEDICINES

To be effective, ear medicines should reach right down to the eardrum. Most bottles and tubes come with applicator nozzles large enough to fit the ear but not so large that they cause damage.

1. Speak to the cat calmly and place it on a table. Wrap it in a towel if necessary.
2. Hold the ear with one hand and insert the nozzle of the ear medicine into the opening to the ear canal with the other.
3. Squeeze the tube or bottle.

Fig. 1: Squeeze the medicine into the ear canal

The cat's head is held firmly.

4. Drop the ear back into place and massage the ear canal. (A squelching sound means the medicine is being thoroughly massaged in the canal.)

Fig. 2: Massage the ear canal

Rub the area below the point where the ear meets the head.

5. Hold the ear and swab away excess medicine and

debris. (This prevents medicine from flying everywhere when the cat then shakes its head.)

6. Praise the cat and give it a food reward.

Never use proprietary wax removers if there is a risk that the eardrum has been ruptured.

HOW TO GIVE INJECTIONS

Insulin injections are usually needed to treat sugar diabetes, but your veterinarian might provide you with life saving medicine to give by injection if your cat is known to go into anaphylactic shock when bitten by wasps or other insects. Giving injections sounds daunting but is quite simple, simpler in many ways than giving medicines by mouth.

1. Draw the medicine into the syringe.
2. Tap air bubbles until they rise to the top of the syringe then expel them until the first drop of medicine emerges from the needle.
3. Restrain the cat on a table.
4. While speaking calmly to the cat, grasp a fold of skin on the neck between the shoulder blades. (This is a relatively insensitive part of the skin.)
5. With a steady movement, insert the needle through the skin into the tissue under the skin and above underlying muscle, then squeeze the contents of the syringe into that space. (Alternatively, your veterinarian may instruct you to give certain life saving drugs directly into the muscles of the hind leg. Follow those instructions carefully.)
6. Praise the cat for obedience and give a food reward.

FIRST AID KIT

It is easy and simple to prepare a first aid kit for cat emergencies. Remember to keep the kit out of the reach of small children.

Bandage material:

- Sterile non-stick gauze pads 7.5 × 7.5 cm (3 × 3 inches)
- Gauze bandage 2.5 and 5 cm (1 and 2 inch) rolls
- Elastic adhesive tape 2.5 and 5 cm (1 and 2 inch) rolls
- Blunt-tipped scissors

Cleaning material:

- Cotton buds
- Absorbent cotton wool
- 3% Hydrogen peroxide
- Tweezers

Other essential items:

- Thermometer
- Sticks for splints (tongue depressors)

Other useful items:

- Needle-nosed pliers
- Blanket
- Transport container

PHARMACY

Coughs:

- Glyceryl guiacolate expectorant − 2 ml every four hours
  (Use a cough suppressant only under the advice and
  supervision of your veterinarian)

Diarrhea:

- Kaopectate − 2 ml per 2 Kg (5 lbs) body weight every
  four hours for one day

Poisoning:

- Activated charcoal (one teaspoon (5 ml) of a thick, watery
  slurry)
- 3% Hydrogen peroxide (one teaspoon (5 ml) every ten
  minutes until vomiting is induced)
- Vegetable oil (one teaspoon (5 ml) by mouth)

Index

Page numbers in *italic* refer to the illustrations

Index

Index

urinating, 52–3, 54–5

vaccination, 159, 162–4
vet, when to take cat to, 31–2
vomiting, 51, 101, 155–6
  inducing, 136–7, *137–8*, 152,
    152

warfarin, 140

wasp stings, 68–9
weight changes, 55–6
weight watching, 169–70
worms, 159, 165–6
wounds: bandages, 21–2
  bleeding, 71–8
  cleaning, 17–20
  foreign bodies, 20, 121
  puncture, 146–9, *148*

FOR THE BEST IN PAPERBACKS, LOOK FOR THE

In every corner of the world, on every subject under the sun, Penguin represents quality and variety—the very best in publishing today.

For complete information about books available from Penguin—including Puffins, Penguin Classics, and Arkana—and how to order them, write to us at the appropriate address below. Please note that for copyright reasons the selection of books varies from country to country.

In the United Kingdom: Please write to *Dept. JC, Penguin Books Ltd, FREEPOST, West Drayton, Middlesex UB7 0BR.*

If you have any difficulty in obtaining a title, please send your order with the correct money, plus ten percent for postage and packaging, to *P.O. Box No. 11, West Drayton, Middlesex UB7 0BR*

In the United States: Please write to *Consumer Sales, Penguin USA, P.O. Box 999, Dept. 17109, Bergenfield, New Jersey 07621-0120.* VISA and MasterCard holders call 1-800-253-6476 to order all Penguin titles

In Canada: Please write to *Penguin Books Canada Ltd, 10 Alcorn Avenue, Suite 300, Toronto, Ontario M4V 3B2*

In Australia: Please write to *Penguin Books Australia Ltd, P.O. Box 257, Ringwood, Victoria 3134*

In New Zealand: Please write to *Penguin Books (NZ) Ltd, Private Bag 102902, North Shore Mail Centre, Auckland 10*

In India: Please write to *Penguin Books India Pvt Ltd, 706 Eros Apartments, 56 Nehru Place, New Delhi 110 019*

In the Netherlands: Please write to *Penguin Books Netherlands bv, Postbus 3507, NL-1001 AH Amsterdam*

In Germany: Please write to *Penguin Books Deutschland GmbH, Metzlerstrasse 26, 60594 Frankfurt am Main*

In Spain: Please write to *Penguin Books S. A., Bravo Murillo 19, 1° B, 28015 Madrid*

In Italy: Please write to *Penguin Italia s.r.l., Via Felice Casati 20, I-20124 Milano*

In France: Please write to *Penguin France S. A., 17 rue Lejeune, F-31000 Toulouse*

In Japan: Please write to *Penguin Books Japan, Ishikiribashi Building, 2-5-4, Suido, Bunkyo-ku, Tokyo 112*

In Greece: Please write to *Penguin Hellas Ltd, Dimocritou 3, GR-106 71 Athens*

In South Africa: Please write to *Longman Penguin Southern Africa (Pty) Ltd, Private Bag X08, Bertsham 2013*